VISIONS
DREAMS
AND HEALING

The Making of a Christian Counselor

R. Charles Bartlett

Acts 2:17 And it shall come to pass in the last days, saith God, I will pour out of My Spirit upon all flesh: and your sons and daughters shall prophesy, and your young men shall see visions, and your old men shall dream dreams.

xulon
PRESS

CONTENTS

⋆⇒◉⇐⋆

Acknowledgements

There are many people involved in almost any project. Certainly that's true with this book. I hope I don't neglect to mention all who have contributed to it.

First, I want to thank the current Self/Rise, Inc. Board of Directors for their encouragement and support - Carole Bergman, Don Brock, Roberta Jacklin, Bob Ruffo, Sandra Stanley, Chip Stembridge, and Phil Vesper. Thanks also to the others who have served in this capacity over the years.

Thanks to the Fort Valley United Methodist Church Harmony Sunday School Class, where I've taught for about 40 years now. Our discussion class has helped me solidify many of the things I've come to believe and has given me a place where I could share freely and openly some of the truths I have learned as a counselor.

It's been great being in a men's Friday morning Bible study group, where we share Biblical truths and their application.

I greatly appreciate the help provided in editing the book by my aunt, Elizabeth Thomas and my granddaughter, Holly DeFore. A special thanks to my daughter Linda Spinks for assisting in preparing the manuscript for submission to the publisher.

Thanks to my grandson, Matt Spinks for urging me to write a book about my experiences.

Thanks to friends who read through the rough manuscript and gave so many good ideas for improvements: Dan Joyner, Dr. Robert E. Wilder and Dr. Joe and Mary Jim Luce.

Thanks to all who have ever contributed to our Ministry in any way.

I am eternally grateful for the positive response and encouragement from those whose case histories are included in the book, and for their approval for us to share from the transcripts of their healings.

Dedication

This book is dedicated to my wife of 51 years, Mary Hunt Bartlett, for her continuing to put up with me and encouraging me in so many ways, but especially as I headed out on what one of my friends called my "foolhardy venture."

Mary has been more than a helpmate and encourager. With the exception of Jesus Christ, she has been the most positive influence on my life.

During our married life together, the two main focuses of my life have been first, my work at Blue Bird Body Company and later Self/Rise, Inc., our counseling ministry. Mary's focus has always been our family. She sees family as a chain, reaching back into our family of the past and forward into the future through our children and grandchildren. Her mission has been to be a strong link in the chain of our family, and she *is* that strong link.

Preface

Has God ever had a conversation with you? Or, given you a vision of something that happened with one of your ancestors who you know nothing about? Has He shown you what you were feeling when you were in your mother's womb, or at birth? Has he shown you traumatic things that happened to you when you were small of which you have no conscious memory? Has He sent you a message through a dream, and then interpreted the dream for you? Has He shown you a vision in order to bring healing to you? Has He ever revealed to you the reason you were created?

These and other things have been experienced by clients who have come to our Counseling Center for healing. We have provided free Christian Counseling for the past 20 years. God has provided some truly miraculous healings through our Ministry, Self/Rise, Inc. (an acronym for Spiritually Enlightening, Love Fulfilling, Resources Integrated, Self-Examination)

The original intent in writing this book was to share some of these healings to:

1. Show the love, mercy and grace of God.
2. Reveal some truths about the spiritual realm He has shown us.

The book was intended to be about the Ministry and not about me; however, my life and the life of the Ministry are so intertwined it's *impossible* to separate them and make any sense about what's been happening. What God has done in my life has been at the very least as much a miracle as His healings for our clients.

The first part of the book is about my walk with God. The second part has to do with the actual case histories of some of our clients. Interspersed among the case histories are some of the truths the Holy Spirit has revealed.

Not long after I received healing for the fear I had been carrying for most of my life, I wrote about what I had experienced:

THE SEARCH

I asked God to show me who I am.
God is showing me how I've become who I am.

I asked God to fill me with His love.
He is teaching me that I cannot feel love fully
Until I acknowledge all feelings, both good and bad.

I asked God to solve my problem with people.
He is teaching me to solve me.

I asked God to remove all my old hurts.
He is teaching me the value of re-experiencing them.

I asked Him to show me how to love my neighbor.
He is showing me that I have to first learn to love me.

I looked everywhere for God and His Kingdom,
And found it where it always was...
Inside me;
Covered over with the obstructive layers of
My old fear, guilt, anger and insecurity.

As I have sought God's best for my life,
In His infinite wisdom, mercy and grace,
He is giving me, ME!

1.

The Start of My Christian Journey

The *basis* for the miracles which have happened in my own life as well as the miraculous healings that God has brought to hurting people at Self/Rise is my becoming a Christian at the age of 34. Without this base, there would be no Self/Rise.

I believe that before anyone should even *think* about accepting anything anyone shares with them, it's important that they know something about that person; what he believes and why he believes it.

I grew up in Fort Valley, a small town in middle Georgia. It was a great place to call home. Fort Valley had an outstanding school system, where I was an average student. In high school, I was active in literary events and in sports, participating in basketball, football and track.

My brother Gene (two years younger) and I attended the Baptist church. Our immediate family didn't attend church at that time, but they saw that we got to church each Sunday. My grandfather Evans was very active, at one time teaching a group of young men and later, leading the singing at church services. When I was 12, our Sunday School teacher told Gene and me one Sunday it was time for us to join the church. We told him we didn't have any plans to do that. He said, "You believe in Jesus, don't you?" When we said "Yes," he said this was the day.

He sat with us in church and when the altar call was made at the end of the sermon, he pushed us out into the aisle and there was nothing to do but go on down to the front. We were baptized the next Sunday night, along with a number of others. I was not aware of any difference in either of us at that time because of the experience.

There was always work for youngsters when I was growing up. Fort Valley is the peach capital of Georgia and there were enough packing sheds in Fort Valley and in the surrounding area that anyone who wanted summer work could find it. We could easily make enough money in the summers to pay for our school clothing. I also worked in grocery stores and later, I worked several years at an Agricultural Experiment Station and, one summer during college, I worked at Blue Bird Body Company, a manufacturer of school and transit buses.

In high school, I was good enough in basketball to be chosen one of ten players to represent south Georgia on the state all-star team. I was a substitute and got little playing time in the game, but the coach from North Georgia College contacted me after the game and offered me an athletic scholarship. I found later that the scholarship was only for $50 per quarter, provided I put in 100 hours working in the gym. It wasn't much, but as I recall, it only cost $150 a quarter to attend North Georgia at the time.

North Georgia is a military school, where male students wear army uniforms all the time. On Sunday mornings, the cadets were assembled and marched over to the church of their choice. At first, I attended the Baptist church as I had at home, but there was a long-winded preacher there who repeated himself a lot. As soon as I found that a seminary student pastor at the *Presbyterian* Church gave 15-minute sermons, for the balance of my time at NGC, I was Presbyterian.

After my time in service, I married Mary Hunt, who had been teaching first and second grade in Fort Valley. My first job after we married was in sales with Proctor and Gamble, working out of Chattanooga, Tenn. I found that P&G's kind of selling was not for me, so after a month, I resigned, and Mary and I headed back to Georgia. I interviewed several businesses in the Fort Valley/Macon area, but there was little hiring going on at that time. Blue Bird Body Company told me they might be hiring someone soon, but we were out of money and couldn't wait for something to open up there. Mary's father had just bought out a hardware store in Blakely, Ga., and said he needed someone to help him. We moved to Blakely, and I spent almost a year there working with him.

A friend told me there were some jobs opening up at Woolfolk, a chemical company in Fort Valley, so I went up one weekend to apply. There were two openings, one in the chemical plant and another in the accounting office. The salary offered was not as good as I had received at P&G and I told them I'd consider their offer. When A. L. (Buddy) Luce, Jr., President of Blue Bird heard I might be coming back to Fort Valley, he told my mother he'd like to visit with me. I didn't think I wanted to work at Blue Bird, but I had some time left after interviewing at Woolfolk, so I went by to talk with Buddy. He offered me a job paying the same salary I had received with P&G, with a guaranteed raise in six months if everything worked out. The job was in the Production Division, working in the department responsible for packing and shipping parts overseas for assembly of buses in foreign countries. The man in charge of the department was preparing to go overseas to set up an assembly line, and I was to take his place after he left. I went to work on my birthday, April 12, 1956. I had a good crew and worked hard at the job, and the hard work paid off. I got the six month guaranteed raise two or three months after I started work.

Things progressed well in the job through the summer. In the fall, I was told I needed to work through the plant to learn how to set up an assembly line. We had sold a number of buses in Iran and Blue Bird needed someone to go over and assist in setting up an assembly operation. I had not fully worked my way through the plant when I was given the option of continuing to prepare to go to Iran (this was at the time of the Suez Crisis) at Christmas time, or going into the Sales Division as Northeast Regional Sales Manager.

Naturally, I jumped at the chance to let someone else go to Iran. In getting into sales, I bit off more than I realized at the time. The Northeast Region included the eastern half of Canada, the states from Maine down through New York, Pennsylvania, West Virginia, and the states east of those, plus Florida and Texas. In these states and provinces, with the exception of the state of Florida, we sold through distributors. The only distributors we had in the states I'd been given were a few people who, over the years, had applied for a distributorship, so I had my work cut out for me. When I started, we only had six distributors in six of the Northeastern states selling about 130 buses a year. Because of some bad experiences the company had in New York state, we weren't able to do much business there for several years after I took over the region.

My first assignment as Regional Sales Manager was to go to West Virginia to look for a distributor. I had no idea how to do that. When I asked the Sales Manager how to find a distributor, he said I should check with truck equipment dealers and truck dealers to see if there was any interest. Since I would be in Charleston, I was also to go by and visit with the State Transportation people to see if they would have any recommendations for us. I flew to Charleston and started calling truck and equipment dealers on the phone attempting to get an appointment to go out to see them. They all asked what the product was I was representing, and when I said, "school buses," they said, "Forget it!" It took a little over an hour to run through all the prospects I could find in the yellow pages. I went by the state department and visited with the Director of School Transportation to learn what I could. I can't remember how I finally found a distributor, but before leaving the state, I did set up a automotive dealership in southern West Virginia as distributor for the state. It was only after I got back to Fort Valley that I was told Blue Bird had been trying for several years to find a distributor there.

I was green as grass as a salesman and there was nobody at Blue Bird who had the time to travel with me to show me the ropes. It was strictly on-the-job training and I made a lot of mistakes. My second trip was to Somerville (a suburb of Boston), Massachusetts. Our Sales Manager, George Mathews, had heard that the Oneida (a New York bus manu-facturer) distributor, Walsh Body Company, was considering dropping Oneida and going with another manufacturer. He contacted the folks at Walsh Body and set up an appoint-ment for me to see them. The General Manager and his Sales Manager met me at my hotel for supper. After supper, they asked about our prices. I told them that since Walsh was a competitor, I wasn't sure I could show them our prices, but I would call my Sales Manager and if he said it was okay, I would go over the prices with them the next day. When I called George, he was very emphatic. His exact words were "Hell yes, show them our prices!" And I was to show them anything else they wanted to see. I think this gives you some idea how green I really was, but I *was* successful in signing Walsh Body and they became a good distributor for us.

Blue Bird believed in helping their employees learn in any way they could. I hadn't been in Sales long before they sent me to a sales training seminar in Atlanta. As I recall, this was early in 1957. When I checked into the hotel, I found

I had been roomed with the Sales Manager of the Texize Company. He was a real pro. I explained to him I was new in sales and would appreciate any suggestions he might give me on how I could learn to be a good salesman. He had one piece of advice: "Teach Sunday School at your church." He told me that was an excellent way to learn to think on your feet, and it would put me in a position where I would learn what I really believed.

Following his advice, not long after I got back home, I started teaching in our local Methodist Church. Churches are usually so desperate for teachers, most are willing to let almost anyone who applies teach. I started with teenagers, but quickly found I wasn't gifted for teaching that age group, and stopped teaching for a time. Later, I started teaching adults, about my age. I figure I've been teaching adults in the Fort Valley United Methodist Church for about 40 years now. I realize today the reason I wasn't successful with the teenagers was because I was trying to teach out of my own strength, since I wasn't a Christian.

As I've already mentioned, when my brother and I were growing up, we went to church because it seemed to be the thing to do. After getting married, it continued to be the thing to do. Since Mary was a Methodist, and I didn't really care which church we attended, we started attending the Methodist Church, and I joined as a member. As our children came along, Linda in 1958 and Genie in 1960, we went to church as a family.

Going to work at Blue Bird when I did was a fantastic experience. Up until that time, Blue Bird had been a regional company selling mostly in the Southeastern states. Management had decided to start setting up a nationwide group of distributors and during the time I was with them, we were able to bring together a group of distributors who would take us to the number one position in sales in the U. S. and in Canada.

My job required extensive air travel, and I don't think it would be stretching it to say I traveled 100 days a year. If there was a single event that caused me to start thinking of seeking a relationship with Jesus Christ, it was one prompted by a friend, Len Lorber. Len was a Superior Coach distributor in New York state who I'd gotten to know when I was traveling in western New York. I liked Len a lot and was impressed with the way he did business and had hoped that someday, I might be able to convince him to leave Superior and come with us. In 1964, he stopped by the plant on his way to Florida on vacation. We were visiting in my office, discussing the bus business, when, out of the blue, he said, "Charlie, you're a Christian, aren't you?" His question offended me. I thought to myself, "Why did you have to bring that up while we were discussing business?" I answered, "Yes, I go to church," and he said, "Great!" and then we continued our talk on business. His question had been like a blip on a screen.

After Len left, I was perturbed by his question. My thinking went something like this: "If someone asked me if I was a man, my answer would be "Yes," because I know I'm a man. Why could I not answer his question emphatically when he asked if I was a Christian? If I wasn't certain, maybe I wasn't one." (In looking back on this, I know God prompted Len to ask me the question. A number of years later, after I became a Christian, I called Len to thank him for asking me the question that day. He said he was happy if that had happened, but he had no recollection of asking the question.)

Although I had attended church most of my life, I didn't know how to become a Christian. My first reaction was to try to get "good enough" so I would be acceptable to God. That didn't work. The harder I tried to be "good" in my own strength, the more that quality eluded me.

I had to travel extensively by air and don't remember ever being at ease on airplanes. From the time the flight started until it ended, my hands and feet would sweat profusely, and my heart would jump into my throat whenever I experienced anything other than a smooth flight. To add fuel to the fire, it was about this time that airlines started having trouble with Lockeed Electras, a popular plane of that period. There was a basic flaw in those planes at the base of the wings, and at times, wings would come off planes in flight and all the passengers would be killed. Having been brought up in the Baptist church, it had been programmed into me that there *is* a hell. I knew if I was ever in a plane crash and wasn't a Christian, I wouldn't stop at the hole in the ground made by the crash- I'd continue on down to hell. That made my trips even more stressful, and it finally got so bad, I gave thought to considering some non-traveling work.

One of the first times God revealed Himself to me was in a motel where I was staying in Burlington, Vermont. Although I had heard about God all my life, I didn't know whether He really existed. I was getting desperate to know if He was real. That night, I got down on my knees by the side of the bed and prayed this prayer, "God, if You are real, would You please reveal Yourself to me?" When I opened my eyes, nothing had changed. In frustration, I cut off the light and turned over in bed. As I turned over, my fingers rubbed across the headboard, and where my fingers had touched, there was a streak of light. I thought, "I don't believe I saw that!" But, every time I rubbed my hand across the headboard, the streak of light reappeared. My first reaction was to rationalize it must have been static electricity. As I've looked back on this, I now realize it was God's answer to my question. In all the motels where I stayed in the 30 years I traveled, it had never happened before and it never happened again.

This, and other things that have happened in my life, have convinced me God is real and He doesn't mind our putting out "fleeces" in order to get direction or answers or to know something is from Him. Looking back on my life, I can see many times that God's hand has guided me, when at the time, I didn't realize it. There have also been times when the thing that happened was so dramatic, I knew immediately it was from God.

One Monday morning, I was walking down the hall in the Sales Division when I saw George Luce (one of the owners of Blue Bird) coming toward me. George asked if I was leaving town that day. (It was normal for us to start our trips on Monday since the company didn't want us to travel on Sunday if we could help it). I told him I was, having planned to fly out of Macon to Atlanta, where I would pick up my connection. He asked if I'd like to ride up to the Atlanta airport with him, since he also had a flight out that day. I quickly agreed. A ride to Atlanta always beat catching the commuter flight out of Macon and connecting in Atlanta.

As we got ready to leave, the thought came to me that George would be a good one to ask about becoming a Christian. George had been an industrial missionary in Africa before coming back to help run the family business. We hadn't reached the city limits of Fort Valley when I asked George the question: "George, how do you become a Christian?" He had his Bible with him and had me read several passages from it. The verses he gave me didn't really answer my question. He started speeding up and kept watching his rearview mirror to be sure there wasn't a highway patrolman behind us. He said he was trying to make up some time so we would have time to have a prayer before we got to the airport. We stopped this side of Atlanta, and George prayed for me and then asked if I wanted to pray. I prayed, telling God I repented of my sins and asked Jesus to come into my life. After my prayer, George asked if I felt any different. I told him that honestly, I didn't. He said that didn't matter, that I had done all I needed to do and I just needed to accept on faith that Jesus had come into my life.

Just the two of us had never been in an automobile together before, and in the remainder of my time at Blue Bird, it never happened again. Our spending that time together that day had to be the work of God.

When I boarded my flight that day, I said, "God, I've turned my life over to You. George told me that would do it. I'm going to let You have responsibility for what happens on this flight." For the first time, my hands and feet didn't sweat and I knew that I was now different. The date was April 19, 1965, 7 days after my 34th birthday.

Becoming a Christian, as I'm sure you know, brings on a lot of learning experiences. One of the first things I learned was that not everyone is as excited about what has happened to you as you are. When George took me to Atlanta, I was on my way to visit our distributor in New Jersey. The salesman I was to work with that day and I had become pretty good friends, not close, but we could talk about a lot of things. We were in his pick-up, on the way to make a sales call on a customer, when I started telling him what had happened earlier that day. As I started telling him, I became aware of a wall going up between us. He got real quiet and we didn't talk much after that. There's a scripture that tells us to "not cast our pearls before swine." God has a sense of humor. The salesman's nickname was "Piggy."

On my trip, God did provide someone I *could* share with and the reaction from him was positive. So, I became a Christian 22 years after my brother Gene and I had been baptized in the Baptist Church. Gene was living in Melbourne, Florida, and the next time I saw him, I told him about what had happened. He told me he, too, had also recently become a Christian. We talked about this, and Gene felt that although when we had joined the church, it did not mean anything to us, God honored what we had done and had His hand on us all those years. Later, our Dad joined the Baptist Church because, as he told Mother, "I want what Charles and Gene have." He later became a deacon of the local Baptist Church, one of the high points of his life.

Somewhere around this time, there was a movement in the Methodist Church called Lay Witness Missions. I got involved in these missions for a period of time, and went with groups to be one of the witnesses at other churches. This gave me a chance to witness what God was doing in my life. We were always well-fed and housed with church members and were constantly being told what great people we were to come. It finally got to be too much of an ego trip for me, and I decided to seek other ways to serve. In addition, I was not giving enough time to Mary and our family. I was having to travel a lot with Blue Bird, and attending these Missions on week-ends took even more time away from them.

I can't remember exactly when Mary and I started going to Bill Gothard's Institute in Basic Youth Conflicts in Atlanta. These Seminars, which went on over the period of a week, were held in large arenas because there were usually somewhere around 20,000 people in attendance. One of our Sunday School members attended, and was on fire for what was being taught by Gothard. I asked him to share with the class what he had learned. There were some things he shared I didn't agree with, but over time, I noticed a lot of positive changes in him.

The next time Gothard came to Atlanta, I told Mary we would go up for the first night, and unless it was really good, we wouldn't attend for the remainder of the week. The Basic Youth Conflict sessions were held on Monday through Thursday nights and all day Friday and Saturday. We were so impressed with the things covered that first night, we drove up for the other sessions. Gothard had the gift of being able to explain the *practicality* of Christianity in a way I had never experienced it before.

Mary and I were so impressed with the Seminar we started talking about it with friends, suggesting they consider attending the next time it was offered in Atlanta. We came up with enough people for a bus load. I asked Joe Luce if we could use one of the Blue Bird school buses for the trip, so people wouldn't have to drive up in separate vehicles. Joe said if we could get enough people to go, he would provide a Greyhound coach for those who wanted to attend. We ended up with *three* coaches filled with people. At the Seminar, Gothard did two chalk drawings. At the end of the Seminar, he gave one of the drawings to the group that had the most people there from the greatest distance. We won that drawing.

For the next few years, Mary and our daughters and I attended every time Gothard came to Atlanta. In one of the early sessions we attended, Gothard taught on forgiveness. He said if there was anyone we needed to ask to forgive us for anything, and we had lost contact with them, we should tell God that we would work up the words to say in asking for forgiveness, and, if He wanted us to ask for forgiveness *in person*, He would cause our paths to cross so that we could do it. The only thing that came to my mind was an incident in high school when a friend, Mary Ann Slappey, asked me about something she had heard I had said, and I denied having said it, knowing I was lying through my teeth. This may seem a minor thing to you, but I wasn't in the habit of lying and felt very guilty for what I'd done. Before we graduated from high school, Mary Ann and her family moved away from Fort Valley and I didn't see her again until my second year at North Georgia College when she came to school there. She married Marvin Doster, a classmate. After leaving college, I lost track of them.

I prayed the prayer that Gothard had suggested, that, if God wanted me to ask Mary Ann to forgive me, He would cause our paths to cross. At the very next break in the Seminar, I went out to get some materials and, as I started back to my seat, someone called out, "Charlie Bartlett!" It was one of my roommates from college- Burt Fargason. Burt was headmaster of a school in Alabama. He invited me to come meet his wife and two sons. After I met them, Burt said that since the next day was an all-day session, he and his family were planning to bring a picnic lunch. He asked me to bring Mary and have lunch with them. I told him we would. You can imagine my shock when, as I started to go back to the section where we were sitting, Burt said, "By the way, Marvin and Mary Ann Doster are here and will also be having lunch with us."

When we met the next day and I asked Mary Ann to forgive me, she didn't remember the incident, but graciously forgave me. As I thought about the fact that there were somewhere around 20,000 people in attendance at the seminar and considered the odds against Mary Ann and Marvin even being there, I knew it was not just circumstantial that the one person I wanted to ask forgiveness from was available. I knew God must have caused this to happen for a purpose.

After we got back home, I decided to teach our Sunday School class what I had learned about forgiveness. I was working on that lesson when God spoke to me clearly:

"HOW CAN YOU TEACH A LESSON ON FORGIVENESS WHEN THERE ARE SO MANY PEOPLE YOU FEEL SO HARD TOWARD?"

I honestly had no idea who He was talking about.

"Lord, who are these people I feel so hard toward?"
"ALL THOSE FORMER FRIENDS WHO PULLED THEIR CHILDREN OUT OF THE PUBLIC SCHOOLS WHEN INTEGRATION CAME. DON'T YOU REALIZE ALL OF YOU WERE TRYING TO DO WHAT YOU THOUGHT WAS BEST FOR YOUR CHILDREN?

Immediately, I realized how judgmental and wrong I had been.

When the public schools were integrated in Georgia, many parents agonized over what they should do for their children as far as the next school year was concerned. Mary and I spent a good bit of time trying to decide what would be best for our daughters. Figuring that one of the important aspects of going to school is learning how to get along with others, we decided the best thing to do was to keep Linda and Genie in the public schools. A number of our friends decided the other way and pulled their children out of the public schools to send them to private schools, which started popping up all over. I took up an offense against some of those former friends, who I felt had deserted the cause. It's embarrassing to admit how I felt and how I acted about this, but I can remember times when, if I was walking downtown and one of those former friends was walking toward me, I would cross the street rather than speak to them.

I knew what I had to do, and asked God to give me a list of all those I needed to see to ask for forgiveness. He quickly gave me a list. I worked up the words to approach them with- "_____, God has revealed to me that I have not been as loving a friend to you as I should have been and I've come to ask you to forgive me." Gothard taught that in asking for forgiveness, rather than discussing the *specific* thing we were asking to be forgiven for, we should get to the basic problem. In almost every case, it's a lack of love. By getting back to the basic problem, our asking for forgiveness covers a multitude of sins and might even cover an offense the other person has been carrying against us we didn't even realize we needed to ask forgiveness for. It is a way of getting the slate clean and not leaving any residuals.

Gothard went on to say that, once you ask someone for forgiveness, you *keep your mouth shut*. No matter how long it takes, the person from whom you are asking forgiveness has to say the first words. If he says he forgives you, you thank him. If he says he can't forgive you, you say (only if you can honestly say it), "_____, if I were in your place I think I would feel the same way you do, but can I ask you to do something for me? If you ever find it in your heart to forgive me, would you let me know?" This way, you have done all you can do and the ball is now in his court. You have shifted the burden from your shoulders to his.

I dreaded having to see the people on my list and wanted to get it over quickly so that I wouldn't have to keep dreading it. I picked the toughest one to contact first. He was a friend from high school. I called and asked if I could come out to see him. When I got to his house, we went into his den and I sat on the sofa and he sat on a hassock facing me. I said, "_____, God has revealed to me that I have not been as loving a friend as I should have been and I've come to ask if you would forgive me." He hung his head and didn't say anything for what seemed an eternity. Then he looked up and said, "Sure, I forgive you." I didn't know what else to say, except to get up and thank him. One by one, I contacted the others and all were very forgiving. When I asked one of them to forgive me, He said there was nothing to forgive. I thanked him but told him it would mean so much if he would *tell* me he forgave me. This went on for awhile with him telling me there was nothing to forgive and my thanking him and telling him it would mean so much to me for him to say the words. He finally said he forgave me and I thanked him.

Although this was a very painful experience, it was a fantastic *learning* experience. It has caused me to be very careful to not develop a judgmental attitude about things. Earlier, I said I thought there must have been a purpose in my having the experience of asking for Mary Ann's forgiveness. That first opportunity to ask for forgiveness went so well, it took some of the edge off my concern and fear when I had to approach others.

There were other times when something happened and there was no question it was from God. One of the important functions of my job as Vice-President of Sales was to provide a forecast of our sales for the next year. The Production Division would use that forecast to determine how many parts to manufacture. It was more efficient to run some parts in large batches and store them for future use. We had to constantly adjust the forecast to meet situations in the marketplace, and every time we did, the Production people would moan and groan, because it made more work for them. They were just as upset if we *increased* a forecast as they were if we *decreased* it.

As a green young Sales Manager, I felt guilty every time I had to make a change in the forecast. From the way the Production people reacted, I got the impression that if I was really good at my job, I should be able to hit the nail on the head at the first of the year and not make any changes after that.

Later, I realized that a forecast is just that— an educated guess about what might happen. We based our forecasts on information provided by our Distributors and Salesmen, by statistics provided by the states on previous year's purchases, and by current market conditions.

In late 1977, after we had published our latest forecast, Buddy Luce came back and asked if I felt good about it. He said he realized that if we under-forecast and didn't build buses at a fast enough pace, we would get behind and have a problem making deliveries on time, but if we over-forecast, we would run through all the orders we had to produce and have to let some people go around Christmas time, which the Luces abhorred. I told him I'd recheck the numbers and see if the forecast still looked good. I went back over all the figures and checked and rechecked and kept coming back to basically the same figures. I was still not *totally* convinced because I knew everything I was doing was based on a guess.

I had heard of people opening the Bible with their eyes closed and pointing with their finger at the page, and then opening their eyes and reading the passage and getting a message from God. Out of desperation, that's what I did. I had a Bible on my desk. I closed my eyes, opened the Bible and pointed to a verse. When I opened my eyes, this is what I read, "According to my earnest expectation and my hope, that in nothing I shall be ashamed...(Phil. 1:20)." What is a forecast, but an earnest expectation and hope? If I wasn't to be ashamed, then what I came up with would be correct. I took all this to mean that the forecast was correct. About the time I completed reading this, I saw Joe Luce coming down the hall and told him that the forecast was right and why I believed it. We *did* make the forecast and didn't have to release any workers at Christmas time.

This gives you a part of the background of my early Christian journey.

2.

Starting a Ministry-
Self/Rise, Inc.

I think it was back around 1975 or 1976 when I was leaving on a trip for Blue Bird that something happened that profoundly affected my life. Mary's Dad had driven up to Fort Valley from Blakely and was planning to fly to Cleveland to visit Mary's sister, Isabel. Mr. Hunt drove up to the Atlanta airport with me. His flight left about two hours before mine, and after I got him on his flight, I realized I hadn't brought along anything to read to pass the time.

I went over to the concession stand to see what might look interesting, and there, among *Playboy* and other magazines was a paperback book titled, *Prayer Can Change Your Life*. I thought, "What a strange place to see a book like that!" I was curious and picked up a copy and leafed through it. The book was about a scientific study done at Redlands College in California to determine if it could be scientifically proven that prayer works. The author had used test groups of people with similar problems in his study. I turned to a place where it stated that, at the end of the study, one of members of one of the test groups could still not acknowledge that there was a God *by that name*, but he did acknowledge there was a loving entity who had set the universe in motion and was in control of it. The author of the book said, "And that was okay." I thought, "I don't believe that; you need to call God, *God.*"

I put the book down and went over and sat down. As I was sitting there, the thought came to mind that God has been called by many names. Who was I to say that He couldn't be called by some other name? I got up, went back over, purchased the book and started reading. It was so interesting, I read until my plane loaded, and also on the flight. By the time I cut off the light in my motel room that night, I had read through it.

When I got back home, I mentioned the book to our Sunday School class. They said they would like to study it, so I started teaching from it. While we were studying the book, we learned about "Yokefellow Groups," groups of from eight to 12 people who got together, took a psychological test, and drew a picture of a person. The test and picture were evaluated by Yokefellows, Inc., in Burlingame, California, and twice a month for six months, results (slips) were sent to each person discussing areas of their lives which needed to be worked on, along with Biblical references to those areas. Yokefellow Groups were really talk therapy groups based on a combination of Christianity and psychology.

One of our class members, Roberta Jacklin, asked if we could start a Yokefellow Group. We got the address of Yokefellows and ordered information for setting up a group. We lined up six couples from the Sunday School class and got started. The results were excellent. We saw more personal spiritual growth in that group than we'd seen in any group up until that time.

After that, we started other groups. I don't remember how many we ended up with, but once, we had three groups going at the same time.

The groups hadn't been going long when we received notice that the Burlingame Counseling Center was planning a Yokefellow Facilitator training seminar at a church in Virginia. Mike Pearson, who had been instrumental in starting some of the groups and I signed up and attended. In leading groups, we had gone strictly by the book. Basically what we learned in Virginia was that we had been doing things correctly.

At the training sessions, we were told about a talk on "Primal Integration" that would be offered at the end of the Facilitator session, but since we had other things to do, Mike and I missed it.

Not long after that, we learned that a training program was going to be offered again in Virginia, but this time to train Primal Integration Therapists. Figuring that, if it was from Burlingame, it must be good, I signed up, having no idea what was involved. When I got to the place where the program was being held, the first person I met was a Doctor who had been a medical (bone surgeon) missionary in Africa. When he was forced to retire from the mission field and return home, because he was no longer strong enough to be a bone surgeon, he went back to school and got a degree in Psychiatry. After that, he found there were many problems that he could not heal with his psychiatric training. He had come for the training, hoping to add another dimension to his practice.

The others I met at the training session were mostly preachers, some also the heads of counseling centers. I realized quickly that I had stepped into something over my head. I went to the man in charge and told him I thought the best thing for me to do under the circumstances was to drop out before the sessions started.

He asked me one question, "Haven't you been leading Yokefellow Groups?" I told him I had. "Then you will do okay here, and I recommend that you stay." So, having no other plans for the time and because I had already paid the fee for the seminar, I did stay.

The sessions consisted of first being instructed in the technique of Primal Integration Therapy and then, being paired off. One would be the therapist and the other the client. I was paired with a preacher from Maryland who also ran a counseling center. He agreed to be the client first. He laid back on one of the mats that had been provided. I asked him what I should do. He said he had done some Primal before and could get into it by himself. I could just be there for him and observe.

He immediately got into a place where his right shoulder started hurting. Not knowing better, I started rubbing it. About that time, he slammed his right hand into the wall he was lying next to and said, "Damn it, I told you I couldn't do it!" Afterwards, he recalled that, in the first grade, he had been a natural left-hander and the teacher made him use his right hand. He had to go to the board and write over and over with his right hand, "I will write with my right hand."

When it came my time to be the client, all I got into was a lot of involuntary jerking. It was like the muscles of my stomach were contracting. I couldn't identify where the feelings were coming from. It was that way for me for the remainder of the weekend. We would be taught some more about the therapy and then we would pair off again.

The training continued for three days. In every session where I was the "client," all I experienced was the involuntary muscle contracting and jerking. I was thinking at the time, "If I ever get out of this looney bin, I'll never come back."

But, when I got back home, I noticed some radical changes in my reactions. Some situations that previously had caused me to overreact in anger suddenly no longer mattered. My lack of responding in these situations convinced me that in some relationships where I had thought someone else was the problem, the real problem was *me*. I realized this because when I stopped overreacting, there was no problem.

There were other positive changes. So, the next time there was a training session on the East Coast, I attended. I was trying to find why I did some of the things I did; why I would react to certain situations the way I did and then wonder why I reacted that way. I was attending these sessions for me. I had no plan to become a therapist, but after completing the second session, a member of one of our Yokefellow Groups asked if I would try the therapy with her. I did and it worked and for the first time, I realized God had given me the gift of healing, using this therapy.

I found it took attending three seminars and some written work to be certified as a Primal Integration Therapist. I attended the third training session at Burlingame Counseling Center in California and had the chance to get to know Dr. Cecil Osborne, who had founded the Yokefellow Groups and had been one of those who had discovered the therapy. Dr. Osborne had been minister of the Burlingame First Baptist church for 33 years and over that time, had gotten into counseling. Burlingame Counseling Center had evolved out of his counseling work. I was greatly impressed with Cecil Osborne, one of the finest Christians I have ever known.

It was at Burlingame that I learned where the jerking I had experienced came from. It was from a whipping my Dad had given me when I was about four years old that I had repressed and had no conscious memory of. The details of this are covered in the chapter on "Programming."

After my healing and a considerable amount of written work, I was certified as a Primal Integration Therapist on May 8, 1978.

3.

Charles and His Foolhardy Venture

In August, 1983, at the age of 52, I *should* have felt I had life by the tail. I was Vice-President, Sales of Blue Bird Body Company, an international manufacturer of school and transit buses located in Fort Valley, Georgia. I had held this position for over ten years and my immediate boss, Corbin J. Davis, Vice-President, Corporate Marketing, had just told me he was considering early retirement and asked if I would be interested in being promoted to his position. Sounds like I should have been able to give him a quick "Yes!" doesn't it? After all, for most of my working life, Blue Bird had been the most important thing in my life. The company was owned by the Luce family, and run like a big family, and a *great* place to work. It had provided me with the prestige of a top position in an outstanding company, at a salary many times over the goal I had set for myself when I left North Georgia College with a degree in Business Administration.

As Vice-President, Sales, I was responsible for school bus sales in the United States, for Advertising and Sales Promotion and for Parts Sales and Service. If I accepted my boss's job, I would also have responsibility for Export Sales.

In addition, I would become a member of the Executive Committee, a group of three people under the Luce brothers, having responsibility for the day to day running of the company. The other two members of the Executive Committee were the Vice-President, Corporate Manufacturing, Vaughn Shepley and the Vice-President, Corporate Finance, David Lindholm.

The reason I had a problem coming up with an *immediate* answer had to do with a part-time Christian counseling ministry God had led me into. I'll give you a shortened version of how I was led into this ministry.

In seeking answers to some things about myself that I didn't understand, I discovered Primal Integration Therapy, and in experiencing healing, found I had been given the gift of helping others using that same therapy. Primal Integration Therapy is based on the fact that the *memory* of everything that has ever happened to us is stored within us, but negative things which happened early in our lives, especially traumatic things, are usually not available to our *conscious* memory. When things are too traumatic for a small child to handle, the event is blocked out as if it never happened. By using a deep breathing technique and getting in touch with *feelings*, it's possible to drift back into those early traumatic events which have negatively affected our lives. These events can go back as far as being in the womb. In addition to some clients re-experiencing traumatic events in the womb, a number of other clients have re-experienced traumatic births. With other clients, it may be something that happened later- in most cases between birth and the age of six. By processing these early traumatic events as an adult, and seeing them from a different perspective, healing can occur.

After some subjective training sessions and extensive written work, I was certified as a Primal Integration Therapist on May 8, 1978 by Burlingame Counseling Center in Burlingame, California. After being certified, I started seeing clients on a part-time basis. Usually I worked with them in the evenings and on weekends. Occasionally, when I had clients come from out of town, I would work with them from 6:30 to 7:30 in the mornings and then follow up in the evenings, so that it wouldn't interfere with my work at Blue Bird.

I worked with *friends* on a no-charge basis, but for others, charged the going rate of $35 for a 45-minute session. I had not been doing this very long when God spoke to me very clearly one day while I was waiting for a client to come for therapy. The words that came to me were "**FREELY YOU HAVE RECEIVED, FREELY GIVE.**" If I had been in a cartoon, you would have seen a light bulb appear over my head. Immediately, I realized the truth in what I heard. You see, I got into therapy to help *me,* and I more than got my money's worth in the healing I received. Being able to work with others was a free gift. When the client I'd been waiting for arrived, I told him what I'd heard, and it also rang true for him. He offered to start working on setting up a non-profit corporation so we could provide therapy free of charge. It took some time, but finally, we received our tax- exempt status from the IRS. Now, people could contribute to Self/Rise and get a deduction on their income tax. We chose a Board of Directors from among some of the people interested in the work.

I thought the words I had heard, "**FREELY YOU HAVE RECEIVED, FREELY GIVE**" came from the Bible, but didn't know where or in what context. When I looked it up, the words were those Jesus spoke to His disciples when He sent them out to minister. These are His words from Matthew 10:8: "Heal the sick, cleanse the lepers, raise the dead, cast out devils; *freely ye have received, freely give.*"

From the moment God told me we should freely provide therapy, we never again charged for our work. Our agreement with God is that we look completely to *Him* to provide for our needs. For that reason, we have also never had a fundraiser, and have never asked *anyone* for a contribution.

God also made it clear He didn't want me to "promote" the Ministry, which would have been a natural thing for me with my sales background. He told me He would send the ones with whom I was to work. The way He explained it was, **"IF I DON'T PREPARE THEIR HEARTS, YOU WON'T BE ABLE TO HELP THEM."** So, we haven't advertised and don't even have a telephone listing for the ministry. We *totally* depend on God to provide those with whom He wants us to work.

In training to be a Primal Integration Therapist and later, in working with clients, I learned some things of which I had been totally unaware. As an example, having grown up in a small town in middle Georgia, I had no inkling that so many children are sexually molested. In fact, I was not aware of it *ever* having happened.

It was an even greater shock to find in the first years of working with people, that a large percentage of the ladies with whom I worked had been sexually molested as children and, in most instances, it was not by a stranger, but by a member of their own family- father, step-father, brother, uncle, or grandfather.

Being sexually molested, especially by someone they should have been able to trust, can produce all kinds of negative programming. Going through this kind of experience makes it difficult, if not impossible, to trust others. It can even make it difficult to trust God.

A second, and very important. thing I learned was that a fetus is a living, feeling person *from the moment of conception.* We've worked with a number of people who re-experienced being in the womb and picked up on their mother's feelings through the umbilical cord. I'll discuss this more fully in a chapter devoted to that subject.

Primal Integration Therapy was very effective and we witnessed a lot of healings. Soon, the work load got heavier than I could handle by myself on a part-time basis. About that time, we received notice from Burlingame Counseling Center that a lady from South Africa who had just completed therapy training was seeking employment at a counseling center in the United States. Her name was Tiba Pretorius, a lady of Dutch descent who had previously been a missionary in Hong Kong. We contacted Tiba, flew her to Georgia, and after an interview, offered her a job. She came to work with us, and now, we had a *full time* and a part-time therapist. Tiba was a gifted therapist and fit right in with our center. She was in the United States on a temporary visa and from the day she came, we worked at getting her a permanent visa so she could remain here and continue to work with us. Although we tried everything we could think of, we were never able to get that accomplished, and in less than a year, Tiba was on her way back to South Africa, and we were back to just me.

We had prayed we could get Tiba's visa problem solved and, at the time, I couldn't understand why God hadn't stepped in and answered our prayers. Looking back on it today, I'm convinced there was a *reason* He kept the visa from coming through. I think He wanted to place me in a position where I would have to make a *total commitment* to the Ministry so He could reveal a better way for me to work with people. I'm convinced He would *not* have revealed that better way had I had continued to work at the ministry part-time.

Now, let's get back to the reason I didn't give my boss a quick answer about the promotion he had offered. Although I had to do a lot of traveling in my job at Blue Bird, I'd been in charge of sales for over ten years and could plan my travel around times I had clients coming. If I took my boss's job, I would have to travel in the export market, and those trips were a minimum of three weeks duration. I didn't know if I could take on this additional travel for Blue Bird and continue providing therapy. I took some time off from work and went out to a cabin my wife and I had built about five miles out from town. For three days, I fasted and prayed for God's guidance. My question to Him was simple: "Should I take that job offer or not?" I was only looking for a "Yes" or "No." After three days, I had my answer, and it wasn't the one I was seeking.

"NOT ONLY SHOULD YOU NOT TAKE THAT JOB; YOU SHOULD RESIGN YOUR JOB AND GO INTO THE MINISTRY FULLTIME."

This is a good example of God's timing being different from our own. I had *planned* to give full-time to the ministry after I retired from the company at 65. At that point, I felt I would be in better shape financially to do it, but here God was saying I should do it 10 years earlier than I had planned. Since His calling was so specific, I felt I *had* to respond to it because I had a vision of myself at the end of my life on my deathbed saying, "I had a chance to do something for God, and I muffed it." I couldn't handle thinking that might happen.

My resignation was dated October 18, 1983. Because I knew it would take some time to make preparation for my leaving, I gave a two year notice. After some discussion, the Luces came back and told me that, even though I'd be leaving, they were going to promote me to the new position for the time I would be there. According to my resignation, I would be leaving the company on October 18, 1985. A week or so after handing in my resignation, Buddy Luce came up to my office and told me he had been looking at my personnel file. He said he and his brothers didn't want to do *anything* opposed to God's will, but if I would consider staying with the company until April 12, 1986, I would be 55 and could start drawing early retirement from the company. I agreed to that with the understanding that if I had clients come and I needed to take time off to work with them, I could. Actually, I never had to take any time off.

So, on April 12, 1986 I jumped from a position of great security where I felt I had a great deal of control into a place where I was totally dependent on God. It had always puzzled me why God chose me for this work. It seemed to me He could have better chosen someone with a background in either psychology or theology, and I had no formal training in either. I had never even taken a psychology course in college. I asked Him why He had chosen me. **"BECAUSE YOU WERE AVAILABLE."**

Recently, I saw a sign on a church marquee that seemed to say something similar. It read, "God doesn't choose the qualified, He qualifies the chosen." Just before I left Blue Bird, I was given the following poem from my very close friend, Dan Joyner, an English Professor at Valdosta State College, in Valdosta, Georgia. I treasure his gift.

THE MAGIC MAT

"Such stuff as dreams are made on"

E'en God must wonder at the strangest dreams of men,
Their lives given over to pursuits of passing fame.
First, he who gains his pool, his Rolls, his splendored
home, and then,
Comes he who rules his legions and empires like
Tamerlane.
Such men dream the world's best dreams, we say:
How then to judge the dreams of Charlie B on his last day?

Success was his- power, fame, the world's material cream.
But he rejects the good with which men's lives do teem.
No more goals in the rising tower of management.
No more the lauds of men will be for him fulfillment.
Not laud, not praise comes more to his ears, for it seems

That Charlie now dreams no more of Blue Bird, but of
<u>screams</u>!

Screams, so they say, that rise from fabled magic mats,
On the floor, he coaxes pain from a lonely child, who
'Til now crowded fearing behind an adult's tortured face.
That's the magic he works- pain, screams, but there
is freedom, too.
On mats not soft or warm, not made for wanton pleasure:
Mats cold, hard, but filled, like Charles, with love
in great measure.

To Charles on the occasion of his
Foolhardy venture, April 12, 1986

After leaving Blue Bird, I thought it might be good to go back to college and get a degree in psychology so I'd have more credentials to do counseling. I could have worked out the time to do that, but God seemed to indicate that college was not a part of His plan for me. I felt He was saying He would teach me whatever I needed to know.

I continued to provide therapy just as I'd been taught, and results continued to be good. Then, in 1988, something happened that forever changed the way we work with people. What happened is found in the first case history, the story of John, which we will get to after I explain about programming and how we work with our clients.

4.

Programming

There's a saying about computers which can also be applied to people- "garbage in, garbage out." In the case of computers, this simply means that if faulty data is programmed into a computer, the information coming out of the computer will be incorrect. Human beings are much more complicated than a computer, but, like computers, if they receive bad (negative) programming, especially in their early years, it can have a detrimental effect on their lives until they are healed (re-programmed).

Few, if any, people achieve maturity without having received bad programming somewhere along the line. To put it simply, there are no perfect parents. And, even when parents handle things in a relatively adequate way and are affirming to their children, there are many other people and situations which can negatively affect young lives.

The major part of my personal bad programming stemmed from a single event that occurred when I was four years old. What happened was so traumatic for me as a four year-old that I could not process it, and it was blocked from my conscious memory; however, the *effects* of that one event set up some very negative thinking and reacting in my life.

Because of this programming, I was driven to succeed financially so, hopefully, I wouldn't have to ever depend on *anyone*
for anything. Before I received healing, I usually got to work
at Blue Bird before the rest of my department and continued
to work after the others had gone home. Many nights, I would
return to my office for additional work. In addition, I worked
most Saturday mornings, even though the plant was closed.
I put in all that time hoping that, just by hard work and long
hours, I could succeed. As an example of how strongly I was
driven, I think I had a copy of every book on succeeding in
business that had been published at that time.

I also had an unusually strong need for people to like me.
Whenever I was in a group, I always deferred to what others
wanted to do and honestly thought it really didn't matter to
me which option was chosen. One of the ways I determined
if people liked me was if they were accepting of the message
I was presenting. I recall a time when I was speaking to a
group of salesmen in one of our sales training classes and
having the attention of 90% of those attending and finding
myself playing to the ones I didn't seem to be getting through
to. As I look back on it, it doesn't make sense, but at the time,
that's the way I reacted.

When I became Vice-President, Sales at Blue Bird,
although I was manager of many people and knew the value
of getting everyone involved through delegation, *fear* kept
me from ever fully delegating. Although I had not thought
it through at the time, the fear was that someone under me
would make a major mistake, and I would be blamed. It was
irrational, since I had many good people working with me,
but I couldn't shake that fear, which went back to my traumatic programming. In looking back on it after I was healed,
I *realized* it was an irrational fear, but at the time, the way
I operated seemed very rational to me. Before I received
healing, the closest I could come to delegating was to tell
one of my people, "Here is the problem, and here is how we

will solve it." I would then give him in minute detail how I wanted it done, and I would constantly follow up to ensure that he was doing it precisely the way I told him to do it.

You see, at that time, I thought there was only *one* right way to do anything. Later I learned there are lots of right ways to do things, and relatively few wrong ways, but I wasn't thinking clearly at the time because of my programming. After receiving healing for my fear, I realized that those to whom I delegated a problem would probably never solve it exactly the same way I would, but I found many times they devised an even better way than the one I might have proposed. Over time, operating without my irrational fear, it became easier and easier to delegate.

At Blue Bird, where I worked for 30 years, I always received positive annual reviews of my work. My salary increases came faster than I ever expected, and the percentage of my increases was almost always more than the average increase being granted by the company. We were in a period of rapid growth and sales and corporate profits were from good to excellent over the time I was in charge of sales. I had a good team of people who worked well together. In spite of all these positive conditions, I lived with the fear of being fired and having to look for another job. Irrational? Absolutely! The fear had been such a part of my life for so long I never questioned it. I thought that was just the way things were. It all had to do with my programming.

As I previously mentioned, I grew up in Fort Valley, a small town in central Georgia. My family goes back in this general area for at least six generations. At the age of four, I was the first grandchild on either side of the family, and both sets of grandparents lived in Fort Valley. I was spoiled rotten and I'm certain I had come to the conclusion I was the center of the universe .

The year was 1935, in the midst of the Depression and times were hard. At the time, my Dad was about 26 years old. I think there's a good chance he was *programmed* to do what he did because of an incident in his family where his father obviously hadn't been able to control one of my Dad's brothers, to the detriment of the family. I feel fairly certain this prompted my Dad to feel the necessity of getting me under control while I was young so he would be able to handle me when I got older.

At the age of four, I had done something I shouldn't have. I'm not certain specifically what it was, but knowing how spoiled I was, I had probably been insolent, or had sassed my Dad. He told Mother it was time to straighten me out.

In the therapy session where I started to relive this traumatic experience, I had a vision of my grandmother's back porch. We were living in her home at that time. Daddy was standing there with his belt and Mother was there. My grandmother, uncle and aunt were somewhere in the house.

Daddy gave me a few licks with his belt and asked if I was sorry for what I'd done. I said, "No!" Many years later, my Mother asked if I remembered the whipping my Dad had given me. I told her I had no memory of it. She said that he had whipped me and asked if I was sorry for what I'd done, and I kept saying "No," and she said she knew I was just overly excited and didn't know what he was saying.

In re-experiencing this in therapy, I found I *did* know exactly what he was saying and was determined I wouldn't give in to him. After I said "No!," the first time, he gave me a few more licks and again asked if I was sorry. Again, I said, "No!" By the time he started whipping me for the third time, I realized I needed help, so I started yelling, "Somebody come help me! He's killing me!" Nobody came to my rescue. The message I got from this was that people might say they love me, but when I desperately need them, they won't come help me. That caused me to feel I couldn't depend on *anybody* when I got in trouble, and that I'd better do whatever I needed to do to get in a position where I didn't need *anybody.*

The whipping and my Dad's asking if I was sorry continued to the point I became convinced I had no choice but to give in, so I finally said I was sorry, but under my breath, I said to myself, "But, I'll get you back!" This programming set up a series of situations where I would do hurtful things to my parents and, because I didn't know where this attitude was coming from, I would immediately take on a terrible feeling of guilt for hurting those two who were so special to me and who did so many good things for me.

I'll give you just a few examples of some of the ways I "got them back." I attended North Georgia College in Dahlonega, 180 miles from home. Usually, I hitchhiked both ways. North Georgia is a military school and we wore army uniforms, so it was usually fairly easy to catch rides. One week-end, Daddy offered to take me back. When we pulled into my dormitory, one of the tires on the car went flat. I got my things out of the car and went on in, leaving Daddy out there to change the tire by himself. I visited with my room-mates and never went back out to see how he was doing. After he left, I realized what an unkind and unappreciative thing I'd done and felt terribly guilty for not staying with him and helping him change the tire.

Once when Daddy and Mother came up to the college for a Parents' Weekend, when Mother got out of the car, the first thing I did was say something negative about her appearance. She started to cry. I felt terrible about what I'd said, and couldn't understand why I had said such an unkind thing. Later, when I got married, I had wanted my brother Gene to be my best man, but he was in Germany in service and couldn't be there. I asked a cousin to be my best man, and never even *thought* about asking my Dad until I saw him and Mother coming into the church. There was great guilt when I realized I should have asked him. There were many other times when I "got my parents back."

A preacher in California, Paul Ray, and I were in training to become Primal Integration Therapists, and he was working with me when I was healed. Once again, I had a vision of what happened, and at the end of the whipping, I ran over to my Mother and grabbed her, but, for the first time, I was also aware that my Dad broke for the kitchen, which was just off the porch, sobbing like a baby. For the first time, I realized he and I had both been in catch 22 positions. He felt he had to "break" me, and when I resisted as hard as I did, it placed him in a position where he felt if he stopped before he accomplished "breaking" me, he would be setting himself up for not being able to control me when I was older. At the same time, if he continued to whip me, he might permanently harm me physically. It was like there was no way out of the situation for either of us. His crying afterwards was his relief it was all over. At that point, I felt a love for my Dad I had never experienced before. Experiencing all of this as an adult brought the healing I had been seeking.

I don't want to give anyone the impression my Dad wasn't a good man, because he was. He and Mother did an especially good job in raising my brother Gene, my sister JoBeth and me when times were really hard, and they gave us a set of values which continue to serve us today. I could not have wanted better parents than we had.

The results of my healing were dramatic. Back at work, I suddenly found myself delegating most of my job away. We were selling more buses than ever, and it was taking less and less time for me to do my job. I started coming to work at the same time as others, leaving at five and not returning at night. From then on, I stopped going in on Saturdays. The fear of losing my job was gone.

I also came to the realization there were many others on whom I could depend. I had at least six people in key positions who I could always trust to do a good job with what I delegated to them. I no longer felt I had to do it all myself.

And, finally, I came to the point where, although I continued to want people to like me, if they didn't, it was okay. If they liked me the way I was, that was great, but if they didn't, I was not going to change in an attempt to please them. I realized at a deep level that I needed to be *me* more than I needed for people to like me.

My healing was not instantaneous. There were a lot of old habits that started as a result of my early programming that have had to be dealt with. Overcoming these is a lifelong process, but it does get better as time goes by.

Had I not received this healing, I'm absolutely certain it would have been *impossible* for me to respond positively to God when He told me to resign from Blue Bird and go into a faith-based counseling ministry full-time.

53

5.

The Process

Although I am our only therapist and none of our Board of Directors are active in the day-to-day work of the Ministry, many times the pronoun "we" is used when referring to working with clients. "We" refers to the Holy Spirit and me. The Holy Spirit is in charge and leads me. I just try to be open to whatever He wants to do.

I realize the counseling we provide may seem very strange to anyone who has never had a two way-conversation with God. Believe me, I understand. There was a time in my life when I wouldn't have believed it either, and I would have been very *skeptical* of anyone saying they had talked with God. However, for almost 20 years now, we have worked with hundreds of clients who have received help and healing by talking with God, then getting quiet and listening for His answers. I am personally familiar with getting help from Him when *I've* had problems I couldn't solve and asked Him for help. The specific answers I received have made life much simpler and have given me great peace. The help He has provided has also been a great faith builder for me.

Before we start working with clients, we make absolutely certain they know that, as chief therapist, I have no formal psychological or theological training. We have them sign a statement to that effect. We want to be certain we don't mislead a client into thinking otherwise.

Basically, what we do is have our clients ask questions of God and then listen for His answers. We record their conversation with God on a word processing program so that, at the end of the session, we can give them a copy of what was revealed. We've found it can be very helpful to clients to review these transcripts later to recall what they were told and the context in which they were told.

When clients come for their first session, we discuss their situation so that we can better understand what they may be seeking. Sometimes this gives us an indication as to the first questions we may have them ask God.

After getting some indication of where clients are and what their needs may be, we explain the process we will use in seeking answers for those needs. We tell them we will give them the questions to ask Jesus and, after each question is asked, they should relax and see what happens. We ask that clients not *work* at trying to figure out what the answer should be, but to just to simply be open to whatever comes.

Jesus may answer these questions in a variety of ways- with words, impressions, visions, feelings, or possibly a combination of these. I ask that clients to give me whatever comes, even if it doesn't make sense, and to let me know as much as possible about what is going on with them. (I also tell them that one way Jesus may speak to them is through a dream and that, during the time we work together, it would be helpful to share with me any dreams they have in as much detail as they can give me. More details on this are included in the chapter on dreams.)

I ask clients not to question any answers received because if they start questioning, it just slows the process. However, knowing that Satan will often try to come in on the conversation, I tell clients that *I* may question the answer. When that happens, I will have them say, "Satan, I bind you and cast you out in the name of Jesus Christ." Then we will repeat the question to see if the answer received was really from God. We also tell clients that we will be giving them a copy of the conversation at the end of the session, and at that point, they can question the answers to their heart's content. The main thing we are trying to achieve in sharing this with the client is to keep things moving during the process.

We urge clients to continue coming for therapy until Jesus reveals their time here is complete. We've found with many people that once things start getting better, they tend to stop coming. The last case history tells the story of Martha, who persisted in therapy for five years, but when her healing came, it was so complete she was a new person. All the old things in her life which had bound her were gone. Had she stopped coming even a month before the work here was completed, she would not have received the healing she had sought for so long.

We don't want to leave anyone with the impression that when healing comes, there will be no other problems to face. Growing in Jesus is a life-long process. What the Holy Spirit does is give clients whatever is needed to deal with the problems which will come and a peace that can only come from Him.

I end the instructions by telling clients they should not believe anything I or anyone else may tell them. They should not take anything I say for truth. They need to see if it rings true for their spirit before they even think of accepting it. Of course if it doesn't ring true, I tell them they should just forget it.

After a short prayer, we start the client's conversation with God.

One last thing: Having the opportunity to hear God's answers to clients' questions dealing with serious life issues has changed some of the beliefs of this Baptist/Methodist, and I want to share some of these with you. At times, in working with clients, I have received new insights. At other times, something that God has already revealed has been confirmed. While I don't expect or even want you to take my beliefs at face value, it's my prayer that my sharing them with you will cause you to realize there is much more to the spiritual realm than most of us have ever been taught.

6.

Case Histories

The case histories which follow, of necessity, do not include *all* of the information contained in the transcripts of the counseling sessions. If we attempted to share every word of every session, there would not be room to fit them into one book. For example, at least a ream of paper was required to record Martha's sessions. We have tried to glean from the transcripts the basic truths we believe God wants shared.

In sharing these cases, we use the words God, Jesus, and the Holy Spirit interchangeably and give *all three* credit for the answers received even though we may use the specific name of any of the three.

Where we use a pronoun to refer to the Trinity (God, Jesus, and the Holy Spirit), we capitalize the first letter. When we are referring to a specific *answer* from the Trinity, we capitalize all letters of the words in bold type.

The major requirement for counseling the way we conduct it is a direct call from God. We would recommend that no one even attempt to do what we do without a specific calling from Him.

Another extremely important requirement for counseling the way we do it is the gift of the *discerning of spirits* (1 Corinthians 12:10). Often when clients are talking with God, Satan comes in on the conversation and imitates the voice of God (2 Corinthians 11:14). If the counselor does not have this gift of discernment, Satan can either prevent the healing by heading clients in the wrong direction, or he can cause a lot of time to be wasted "running rabbits." If we tried to include in the case histories all the times Satan came in on conversations, it would take away from the basic truths I believe God wants us to share. On a regular basis, we bind Satan and cast him out numerous times during sessions because he doesn't want people healed, and will do whatever he can to prevent healing.

Another requirement for this kind of counseling is being willing to totally depend on God to provide the answers needed. This is a great blessing because it takes the pressure off having to feel responsible for bringing the healing people need. The responsibility is God's and it's great to let Him have that responsibility.

Finally, the counselor needs to have the gift of *not* taking on the burdens of the client. When I'm working with someone going through something particularly painful, I can hurt with them and feel deeply for them as long as we are working, but the minute they leave, I'm able to drop their burden. If I weren't gifted to do this, I couldn't handle the stress.

In working with clients, we give them the questions to ask. We try to use open-ended questions so that, as far as possible, we're not leading anyone to any specific conclusion, knowing that's God's job. An open-ended question at the first of a session may simply be, "Lord, where do You want to start?" or, "What would You like to share with me today?" The next question depends on the answer received.

Before using any case histories for this book, we received permission from each client to use them, with the exception of those with whom we have lost contact over the years. We will so identify those.

Even though a number of these clients have told us they wouldn't mind if their real names were used, the names of *all* clients have been changed for protection. In a few instances, we have also changed some of the minor details about the client.

7.

Alpha- John's healing

John's birth was unusually traumatic. He was delivered breech- his body coming out before his head- and his head was large. In working with him in Primal Integration Therapy (Primal), as he would get into re-experiencing his birth, it was obvious he was in great pain, with his face going through all kinds of contortions. The doctor had such a hard time delivering him that a towel had been wrapped around one of John's legs to try to get traction. The Doctor pulled so hard, the skin was pulled apart. There's still a scar there where the towel was wrapped. Regardless of how we tried to get John "birthed," the pain was always so excruciating that he could not continue. After trying this several times, he finally stopped coming for therapy because he could not handle the physical pain.

About eight years later, he did return. At that point, he was by far the most depressed person with whom I have ever worked. He said his wife, Sara, told him to either get counseling, or she would leave him. After telling me that, he said, "Right now I can't emotionally handle her leaving. All I want you to do is get me strong enough emotionally so that the next time she pulls that crap, I can tell her to leave." The only answer I could think of was "okay."

I had him lie down on our mat, close his eyes, and start the deep breathing technique that we used to get people into their feelings. Almost instantly, he was back in the birth experience, with all the pain that went with it. Suddenly, he opened his eyes, sat up on the mat and said, "If that's all you can do, I'm out of here! This is not going to work!"

In desperation, I asked him to come back the next day, to try something different, honestly not knowing what that might be. Because of his deep depression, I was fearful he might harm himself if we couldn't get him some relief. All I knew was that I *had* to get him to come back, if for no other reason than to buy a little time. He left, promising to come back the next day.

After he left, I started considering what might be done to help him. I recalled that I had worked with several people who had experienced clinical death— where they died and were resuscitated.

One lady had experienced clinical death when she was born. In re-experiencing her birth, she was obviously in great pain one minute, and the next minute seemed to be at peace. At that point, I heard her say, "I'm not going back down there." A few minutes later, she said, "Well, send someone else." Finally, she said, "Then, you go." Immediately, she was in great pain again. At the end of the session, I asked her what had been going on. She said she was talking with someone; maybe it was God. She told Him she was not going back down there. It was too painful. When He said she had to go or **"SHE WON'T MAKE IT,"** she had responded, "Well, send someone else!" He told her He had no one else to send. Finally, she said, "Then, You go!" He told her He couldn't go, but that He would go *with* her.

Also, a month or so previously, we had worked with a lady Youth Minister who had not come for therapy but who did have several personal questions I could not help her with concerning how to relate to a young man she was planning to see at a college reunion. I had suggested she just relax and see if God would answer her questions. As I recall, I told her that it probably wouldn't work, but we would give it a try and see what happened.

It *did* work, and God answered every question she asked. At the end of the session, she said she thought she had made up the answers, but they had a distinct ring of truth to me. Although I had no doubt that God had spoken to her, I had not used that technique again. (And, by the way, the answers she got were obviously the right ones because not long after that, I attended their wedding.)

I thought now might be the time to get God directly involved again. In looking back, I know this idea came from God. It was like so many times, especially as I've grown older, in looking back, I've been able to see the hand of God in my life, when I didn't realize it at the time.

When John came the next day, I told him the only thing I knew to do was to try to get him in contact with God. As I recall, I said, "This probably won't work, but it's the only thing I can think of that might bring you the healing you need." I told him to just relax and I would give him some questions to ask God, and that he should tell me anything that came into his head after the question was asked.

What happened next was so astounding that it changed forever the way we work with people, and it has led me into a lot of new areas of healing and believing. Jesus, God, and the Holy Spirit have been my teacher. While I continue to use much of what I had been taught and had experienced in Primal, I've rejected a significant part of it- not because it doesn't work, but because what God taught me was so much quicker. And, more than that, while Primal primarily deals with *personal* hurts from the person's past- those hurts actually *experienced* in their lives, what God provides not only brings healing from those hurts, but also reveals if there are any ancestral bonds which may have come down through clients' families keeping them and other members of their family in bondage. We'll discuss more about ancestral bonds in a chapter devoted to that subject.

When John experienced positive results in a relatively short period of time, I wondered if this would work for others. It certainly made sense to get hurting people in direct contact with the One who knows them best and Who knows precisely what's needed for their healing. Over time, we found it *does* work with both Christians and non-Christians.

John, then, became the breakthrough case for the therapy we provide today. Although I had always known there was no healing in me and that any healing in Primal had come through the working of the Holy Spirit, I had never called on Jesus, God, and the Holy Spirit to be directly involved with the person as a regular part of therapy until these sessions with John.

To get back to John's situation, when he came, he had hit rock bottom. In addition to his having been forced to change locations and professions, one of his children had been tragically killed in an accident. He and this child had been very close, and after the accident, John had not been able to share his deep grief about his son's death even with his wife, Sara, but had held his feeling in except for times when he would grieve alone. Fortunately for his wife, she had been able to share her grief with John and with others, and deal with it.

Not being able to vent his grief, John became more and more depressed causing Sara to give him her ultimatum.

As we started, I asked John to get as relaxed as he could, and after that, I would give him some questions to ask Jesus. I instructed him to ask the questions out loud and then get quiet and listen for His answer. When something came into his mind, he was to tell me what the answer was, even if it didn't make any sense to him. The first question was, "Father, do You love me?"

After a few minutes of silence, he told me he had heard no thundering voice of confirmation. So I had him ask the question, "Father, why can't I hear Your voice?"

He asked if he should tell me everything that was going on with him. When I said, "Yes," he started sharing what he was experiencing. In his mind, he saw a picture of some great distance, as if he was looking far off, down a corridor. At the end of the corridor, was a bright, white light. Although he was not close enough to the light to feel it, he was aware of being afraid of it. Then, although he was still afraid of it, he moved closer to it. As he came close, the white light spilled all over him and he realized it was not molten heat as he had imagined, but molten *light*. His body was set aglow, as if he had become radioactive. He wanted to run, but didn't think he could. As he moved away from the light, he found he was still glowing.

John thought the light was the love of God, and God was using this illustration to show He loved him.

He had been very small. Now he was growing and becoming bigger than the corridor. It was confining. He continued to grow and the light was getting dimmer or smaller in relation to him.

He started feeling more anger than fear. He wanted to strike out at something.

"Father, why am I so angry?"
"BECAUSE THE LIGHT WENT AWAY BECAUSE YOU ARE GROWING AND GET-TING BIGGER."

John didn't want to hear that. It made him angry that he had to go back down the corridor. He wanted to cry. There was no light in him and he was not strong. He asked God if he could return to where the light was. He could see the light and was looking directly at it.

Suddenly, he became aware of a twisted little creature, not even knee high, standing beside him. He asked, "Who are you?" The creature said, "I am you." John wanted to take him and throw him into the light because it was evident the creature didn't like it. John grabbed him and held him up to the light as he kicked and squirmed.

He told the creature to leave in the name of Jesus Christ. The creature disappeared. Now, for the first time, John could smile at the light, because he had found a use for it. He was not sad now, but at peace and full emotionally. He felt like crying, like this was some kind of release. He felt like lifting his arms. There was no corridor now, just people around the light with their arms raised.

The message John was getting was allegorical. The little creature had been dark, almost charred-looking. He said, "It's interesting, before I left home to come here, Sara and I were in prayer about my coming. During her prayer, she prayed about "the little boy" in me. At that time, I thought her comment a little strange.

"Father, who is that little charred-looking person?"

He could see the creature clearly now. He didn't look human, and when he left, he didn't just walk away, he disappeared.

"Father, why is he so charred?
"THE LIGHT ISN'T GOOD FOR HIM. IT IS TOO PAINFUL TO HIM."

John said if the light was the love of God and the creature didn't like it, the creature was the opposite of it. As he had begun to glow, the creature showed up. He now felt at peace, but felt if he stopped seeing the light and seeing himself as whole, all the good feelings would go away at the end of the session. He asked God if he could continue to see the light and seeing himself as whole when we stopped.

He was some distance above everything. Some people had formed a circle around the light and all had that radio-active glow. These people were large and perfectly formed, and John was one of them. Now, he saw the answer to his question. He realized that he could continue seeing the light and seeing himself as whole *as long as he was a part of that circle*, and that those who were a part of the circle were those who had found the light. He asked who these people were, but got no direct answer.

The first person he saw was a very sick retarded person from his church, and he could also see his wife Sara, and she had a smile on her face- the kind of smile she used to have before she had grown so weary of him and of life. The rest were people he didn't know, almost faceless. He didn't think it was important that he know who they were. He asked, "Father, why are You showing me this group of people?"

As long as he saw the group, it was a shining, perfect picture, but when he started looking at individuals, he started seeing a lot of imperfections. However, as long as the group was together, the light overwhelmed any imperfections. The message John got from this was that he couldn't deal with people outside the light. He also observed that as long as he was away from the light, with no people around, the corridor was very small.

At this point, the session ended. John said, "Wow! What was all that?" I told him I wasn't certain but I had a strong feeling it might possibly be the most real experience he had ever had. Whatever it was, the reality of his healing from God was already evident.

John's second session

A few minutes after we got started, John complained about a slight headache. Then, he said his scalp was flexing, which made his head hurt worse. Suddenly, his head stopped hurting.

In a few minutes, the pain returned. His arms felt tense and his hands and face were beginning to feel warm, as if the sun was shining on them.

"Lord, am I going to have to experience the physical pain from my birth in order to be made whole?"
"YES."

John saw Jesus on the cross. He asked God what seeing Jesus on the cross had to do with the answer He just gave him. The picture of the cross started changing. At first, it appeared Jesus was dead, and the scene had a deep somberness about it. Then, the darkness got lighter and Jesus appeared to be alive. "I think He wants me to come over there. He's beckoning to me." He felt he had no choice but to go to where Jesus was. As he came closer to Jesus, he became aware of a figure between him and the cross. This frightened him, and he ran over and threw himself at the figure of Jesus on the cross.

When he did, Jesus was not there- it was a mirage. Then he saw Jesus on the cross again, and went through the same thing again, except that now, the other figure receded into the background and wasn't relevant any more.

John told God all of this made no sense, and he was starting to get mad; he had started out asking for an answer and nothing God had shown him so far made any sense at all, especially the part about the cross being a mirage. "What does this have to do with *anything*?"

A figure came over and put his arm around John's shoulder. The figure was talking and motioning toward the cross. There were several crosses and they were all empty.

"SEE, WHEN THE PAIN OF THE CROSS WAS OVER, IT WAS OVER. ONE TIME AND I'M WHOLE."

John knew it was Jesus. There was a bright whiteness to Him, and He knew John. They started walking together. Jesus' arm was around John's shoulder.

"PHYSICAL PAIN HAPPENS TO YOU, BUT PUT THAT ASIDE."

He talked with John about the pain involved in what John had done to other people.

"THAT'S LIKE SIN AND IT MAKES YOU FEEL GUILTY, BUT I DIED TO TAKE AWAY THIS GUILT FOR YOU. THE THING THAT IS KEEPING YOU FROM BEING ABLE TO WALK WITH ME ALL THE TIME, AS WE ARE NOW, IS NOT THE PHYSICAL PAIN YOU HAVE EXPERIENCED..... BUT THE WAY...."

At this point, John said he couldn't make out what Jesus was saying.

Suddenly it became clear. Jesus was explaining how the physical pain in John's life wasn't central, and that John couldn't ignore the things he had done to others. It was like, on one side were the things that others had done to him and on the other side were the things he had done to others. The central thing was that the reason he hadn't been able to walk with Jesus like this all the time was because he allowed that stuff to come between them.

"Okay, Jesus, if all those things that have happened don't matter, then I'm just left with the guilt and unforgiveness in me. What can I do? How can I walk with You all the time?"
"THE FIRST THING YOU DO IS PUT YOUR ARM AROUND MY SHOULDER. YOU HAVE TO WANT TO BE WITH ME LIKE THIS MORE THAN ANYTHING ELSE. THAT'S HOW SIMPLE IT IS."

They hugged each other. John said he thought this must be "good-bye," or maybe "hello."

"Jesus, if I want more than anything else to be with You and the other stuff gets less important, will it go away? What happens to those old feeling of mine? Where will they go?"
"DO YOU REMEMBER THAT AS THE WHITE LIGHT WAS POURED OVER YOU, DARKNESS WAS BEING WASHED OUT? AS FOR HOW LONG, OR PERMANENCE, THE RADIOACTIVE GLOW HAS A GOOD ANALOGY IN HALF- LIVES. I WON'T COMPEL YOU TO WALK WITH ME, BUT THIS KIND OF TRUTH WON'T LET YOU BE DRAWN ANYWHERE ELSE."

John asked if he could leave those feelings there and walk with Him.

"WELL, YOU HAVE A BIG HURDLE THERE. YOU ARE GOING TO HAVE TO TALK WITH ME A LOT WHILE YOU ARE HERE."

With those words, Jesus walked off. John felt loose, almost double-jointed.

John's Third session

John could see himself out in the country, on a hillside, and there was a big rock jutting out from the hill. The ground was very steep, and loose rocks covered the ground. There were no trees. He was leaning against the rock waiting on something. He had an assurance that whatever or whoever he was waiting for would be along soon. After he had been there for awhile and nothing happened, he started to get impatient.

"BE STILL!"

John started to take a step but began slipping because of the steepness of the hill and the loose rocks. A hand grabbed his arm and prevented him from falling down the hill. It was Jesus, and He started explaining why He had to teach him on such an elementary level. He told him that when he started to walk on his own, he would have fallen if He had not caught him.

"THINGS WILL HAPPEN WHEN YOU ARE MOVING."

John took that to mean that he had to try things.

"MY SON, YOU DO NOT REALLY KNOW ME AND WHAT A RELATIONSHIP WITH ME CAN BE LIKE. THERE IS A LOT MORE YOU NEED TO LEARN ABOUT ME."

Then, Jesus started explaining to John how He could be both John's brother and God at the same time. They were sitting, and Jesus had his arm around John. John's head was resting on His chest: He was crying and Jesus was consoling him, but John didn't know why he was crying.

"SOME THINGS ARE COMING OUT WITH YOUR TEARS. YOU DON'T NEED TO TALK ABOUT IT, AND YOU DON'T NEED TO KNOW WHY YOU ARE CRYING. YOU CAN JUST LOOK ON THIS AS A MEASURE OF MY LOVE FOR YOU."

John stopped crying and hugged Jesus.

"NOW WE CAN TAKE A WALK."

They walked down a small ravine. He asked Jesus what this place was. There was something that seemed to be alive about the ravine, and there seemed to be something going on, but he couldn't tell what it was. It was like the things that usually concerned him or frightened him no longer affected him.

"NOTHING CAN TOUCH ME, AND NOTHING CAN TOUCH YOU EITHER. HOW DOES THAT POWER MAKE YOU FEEL?"

John just smiled and his chest swelled.

They had walked through the ravine and were standing on a high spot overlooking a grassy arena. John asked Jesus what this place was, but Jesus didn't answer. The arena was empty and they were moving around the top edge of it. Then, down in the arena, things started growing up through the grass. They were plant-like things, but very strange. They were stalks with stuff on them like snapdragons, but without color. John and Jesus sat down at the top, and watched the scene below. The floor of the arena was now covered with those plant-like things. When the plants had started growing, they looked grotesque, but now that the arena was solid with them, they had become like a carpet, and there was no sense of grotesqueness. John asked what all this meant. Jesus was talking and pointing back toward the ravine they had walked through.

As John watched, the ravine closed together and he realized that if he had been there when that happened, it could have destroyed him. He wondered if the things in the arena could also destroy him.

Jesus got up and walked through the stuff in the arena. He stood in the middle, facing John, holding His arms out to him. John didn't know if these things could hurt him, but he *knew* he had to walk out to Jesus. He walked out to Him, and now, he could hear Jesus' words,

"THESE ARE THINGS YOU'VE WALKED THROUGH BEFORE, AND BEFORE, THEY HURT YOU. BUT WHEN YOU WALK THROUGH THE SAME THINGS TO JOIN ME, THEY ARE NO THREAT TO YOU. NOW, WE CAN WALK OUT TOGETHER."

They went back where they were before, and as they did, all the stuff in the arena started going away. Jesus continued to talk with John about the God and brother thing.

"IF IT THREATENED YOU, AND I KNEW IT WAS REALLY A THREAT TO YOU, AS GOD, I HAVE THE POWER TO MAKE IT GO AWAY, BUT BECAUSE I AM YOUR BROTHER, I WANT TO SHOW YOU HOW TO GO THROUGH IT ALONE."

He said that because He had the power to create and destroy, He was God. This was a power that John could never have, but he could learn to make the world powerless. Jesus was very intense about this. He really wanted John to understand this God and brother thing.

"THE ONLY REASON I CAME HERE TO TEACH YOU AND WORK WITH YOU LIKE A BROTHER IS BECAUSE I LOVE YOU SO MUCH AND I WANT YOU TO BE FREE OF THAT FEAR AND SUFFERING. YOU WERE NOT MEANT FOR THAT."

Jesus was sitting and John was laying on his side, looking at the sky and began to think of heaven, even though he knew it was not in the sky.

"NO, YOU ARE NOT SUPPOSED TO UNDER- STAND THAT NOW.
"Jesus, my son is with You, isn't he?"

For the first time, Jesus answered him, starting with his name,

"JOHN, HE IS NO LONGER YOUR SON. HE'S LIKE THOSE BRIGHT AND SHINING PERFECTED CREATURES I SHOWED YOU IN THE CIRCLE."

"Jesus, I miss him so!"

He told John it was all right to miss him and feel bad about it.

"But, Jesus, if you don't want me to hurt, why am I hurting so much?"

Jesus just put His arm around him. It was at this point someone else joined them, and for a moment, he didn't know who it was. Then he realized it was Sara! Jesus knelt in front of them, reached out to them and said,

"THE ONLY THING I CAN GIVE YOU FOR YOUR GRIEF IS EACH OTHER. YOUR SON WAS YOUR COMMISSION, AND NOW I HAVE OTHERS FOR YOU; BUT, IT MUST BE THE THREE OF US."

They stood and hugged and then walked out into the middle of the arena. There was bright sunshine, like a bright spotlight on the three of them. John had a strong feeling of oneness. Jesus was talking about the light and the fact that the light was power, and the power was the three of them. He told them that even when they didn't see the light, it was still on them.

"THERE WILL CONTINUE TO BE THINGS THAT WILL HURT YOU, BUT THE POWER IS ALWAYS THERE TO PROTECT YOU, IF YOU WILL JUST CALL ON IT."

There was a way out of the arena that John hadn't seen before. Up on the other edge was a gate. The three walked toward the gate, Sara and John in front, and Jesus behind with his hands on their shoulders. Jesus told them there was just the three of them now, but the larger the circle became, the stronger it would become.

He bid them farewell. Jesus stood there watching them leave. After they had walked some distance, John looked back. Jesus was still there, and next to Him was their son. They were both waving.

John wanted to return to them, but Sara knew they had to go on, so she gently put her arm around his shoulder and turned him back around. Jesus and their son went back into the arena.

John's Fourth Session

John was standing by a small stream, more like a brook, about four to five feet wide and shallow. The stream bed was covered with smooth rocks and the water was very clear. He was in a clearing, but back upstream, there seemed to be a lot of brush. Downstream, it was covered over again. He was just standing there. Every once in a while, he would pick up a rock and throw it. Then, he picked up several pretty ones and was looking at them when Jesus walked up on the other side of the stream.

"GOOD MORNING! WHAT ARE YOU DOING?"
"I am looking at some rocks."
"WHAT DO YOU SEE?"
"Well, they are hard, angular, heavy, cold, wet, and clean because they have been washed by the water."
"ARE THEY CHANGED BY THE WATER?"
"No, just worn down."

Jesus pointed to a group of plants growing in the water.

"SEE THOSE WATER PLANTS?"

John and Jesus considered the water plants and the rocks. John thought, "Why am I having to be told such simple things?" Jesus smiled and told John that's how simple it really was, but that John tried to complicate things.

"THE ROCKS ARE HARD AND UNYIELDING AND THE WATER WEARS THEM DOWN OVER TIME. THE REED MOVES AND IS ALIVE AND THE WATER ONLY CAUSES IT TO GET BIGGER AND STRONGER. YOU'VE BEEN A ROCK, AND I WANT YOU TO BE A REED."

Jesus held out his hand to John. John took it and jumped across to the other side of the stream.

"Jesus, how do I become a reed?
"IT'S IMPORTANT FOR YOU TO NOTICE THAT ALTHOUGH THE REED HAS ROOTS IN THE EARTH, IT IS AFFECTED BY THE AIR AND THE WATER AROUND IT. THE GROWTH TAKES PLACE IN THE PART YOU CAN SEE. I KNOW THIS IS SIMPLISTIC, BUT IT'S A TRUTH YOU NEED TO BE AWARE OF, AND ONE WHICH CAN BE APPLIED TO YOU."
"Jesus, how specifically do I need to see the application of this? Show me what I need beyond platitudes."
"WHEN THINGS COME UP THAT YOU NEED TO TAKE ADVANTAGE OF OR RESPOND TO

IN A CERTAIN WAY, WE CAN HANDLE IT AT THAT POINT."
"But, Jesus, I think I need something to really get into the center of me- to change my attitude."
"HERE'S THE ATTITUDE YOU NEED TO CHANGE."

Jesus put His arm around John and drew him to Him.

"DON'T WORRY ABOUT IT."
"But that is frustrating! It seems to me that when we talk about the rock and the reed, there must be things I need to know and need to change about me. There must be things that I am going to need to know."
"THE REED DOESN'T KNOW. THE REED JUST IS. STOP TRYING TO THINK ABOUT *DOING*. JUST REMEMBER WHO YOU ARE AND REJOICE IN THAT, AND YOU ARE A REED. YOU SEE, JOHN, ALL YOUR LIFE, YOU'VE WANTED TO CONTROL. ALL YOUR LIFE YOU'VE THOUGHT YOU COULD DO, AND YOU HAVE, BUT NOW, THAT'S WHAT YOU HAVE TO GIVE UP. TO COME UNTO ME, EVERYONE HAS TO GIVE UP SOMETHING. YOU HAVE TO BE WILLING TO LET THINGS GET OUT OF CONTROL, AND COME TO ME FOR A SENSE OF CONTROL. I'VE BEEN GIVING YOU THE MESSAGE OF FREEDOM, AND YOU'VE NEVER UNDERSTOOD IT. YOU DON'T BELIEVE IT. FREEDOM MEANS YOU CAN STOP *DOING*."
"Jesus, I've wanted to be free. I believe in that freedom and have known that it must be the most fantastic thing in the world, but I thought it was someplace else."

Jesus explained how John could walk with Him all the time, and why what He had shown him was important and how different things could detract him from walking with Him.

"YESTERDAY, I SHOWED YOU THAT NOTHING CAN HURT YOU. TODAY, I WANT YOU TO UNDERSTAND THAT PART OF YOUR LIFE WHERE YOU DISTRACT YOURSELF."

Jesus was putting it in terms of the things John did because he needed approval. He told John that the only approval he needed was His, and he already had that.

"Jesus, does this mean I ignore the rest of the world? I know people who claim to be wrapped up in You, but go around hurting other people."
"FIRST, DON'T WORRY ABOUT THOSE PEOPLE LIKE THAT. HERE IS MY DIRECTION FOR YOUR INVOLVEMENT. IN THE PAST, YOU CHOSE WHAT YOU WANTED TO DO. NOW, I WILL CHOOSE WHAT YOU DO."
"Jesus, how will I know it is from You and not from me?
"BECAUSE YOU WILL BE TALKING WITH ME. NOW I WANT YOU TO THINK ABOUT WHAT I'VE TOLD YOU AND SHOWN YOU, BUT DON'T PUT YOURSELF IN A BOX, AND DON'T PUT ME IN A BOX. YOU'VE ONLY SEEN A VERY SMALL PORTION OF WHAT I HAVE TO REVEAL TO YOU."

John asked Jesus what he meant by placing himself or Jesus in a box.

"DON'T TRY TO FIT YOU AND ME INTO THE WORLD THAT YOU KNOW BECAUSE NEITHER OF US IS ANYMORE OF THE WORLD."

John and Jesus went back to the stream and drank, cupping their hands to hold the water. As Jesus left, He said,

"YOU NEED MORE TIME NOW FOR YOU AND THE HOLY SPIRIT TO THINK ABOUT WHAT I'VE SHOWN YOU."

John's Fifth Session

John's spirit left his body. His body was lifeless and he was above it, looking down on it. He was relaxed and peaceful. He felt Jesus was around somewhere, but couldn't see Him. He had a feeling his physical body was becoming more remote. He asked Jesus what was going on.

"THIS IS ANOTHER WORLD."

That was frightening to John. He began to realize it was a world without forms and shapes. He felt he was losing all points of reference. This was something he didn't know anything about. Then, things started turning lighter. He could see a place, and he was there, but he couldn't see himself. There was a sense there were others there, but he didn't actually see anything.

"Now, I'm being asked to consider the great distance from where I am to the body below. What I'm hearing is that in this place, I'm free from all the trappings that go with the life of the body and material things."

"Jesus, what goes on in this realm?"

"**WHEN YOU SAY REALM, YOU ARE THINKING THIS MIGHT BE A PLACE LIKE EARTH. THERE IS ONLY ONE REALM. WE ARE JUST IN A DIFFERENT PART OF IT. YOU ARE NOT IN HEAVEN. YOU ARE SEEING ANOTHER POTENTIAL FOR HUMAN EXISTENCE.**"

"I'm still not understanding what goes on here, Jesus."

"**THIS IS A PLACE OF PREPARATION.**"

"But, how can I grow and prepare when there's nothing going on?"

"**YOU ARE STILL CONFUSING THE PLACE WITH WHAT IS HAPPENING. THIS IS A SPIRITUAL APARTNESS, A DIMENSION THAT IS FREE FROM THE PHYSICAL WORLD, BUT IT'S NOT AN END UNTO ITSELF. IT IS A MEANS FOR YOU TO DRAW CLOSE TO ME, TO GROW CLOSE TO WISDOM AND TO GROW CLOSE TO STRENGTH. SINCE OUR LAST VISIT, OVER THE WEEKEND, WHEN YOU WERE NOT PUTTING YOURSELF WHERE I AM, YOU BECAME DEPRESSED. YOUR DEPRESSION COMES TO YOU FROM THE WORLD. YOU ACTUALLY HAVE TO DRAW AWAY FROM THE WORLD IN ORDER TO BE IN MY PRESENCE.**"

John thought he was hearing that in this situation, state, condition, there weren't any shapes, but there were other beings around. He felt there was some potential for communicating with these spirits or other people, and there was strength and growth. He thought he was beginning to understand where he was, but it was very frustrating.

Now, he and Jesus had form and were hovering close above his body. Jesus reminded him that when he first moved into the white area, he was relaxed and at peace and looking forward with anticipation to what was coming, and he became frightened when he couldn't make it fit with what he was familiar with.

"YOU BROUGHT TOO MANY CONCEPTS, TOO MANY PRECONCEIVED IDEAS WITH YOU. YOU DON'T KNOW HOW TO GET THERE WITHOUT THEM."
"Am I going to have to give up all my pre-conceived concepts and ideas?"
"WHEN IT COMES TO UNDERSTANDING THE SPIRIT, YOU ARE TRYING TO COMPLICATE IT TOO MUCH. YOU HAVE TO SEEK THE CLEAR AND VOLITIONAL SEPARATION OF THE SPIRIT AND THE PHYSICAL. YOU HAVE TO SEEK THE APARTNESS."
"Why am I being shown the drawing away to another place when I've been taught that You're here in the trenches with us?"
"THE DRAWING APART IS NECESSARY. I HAVE COME BACK WITH YOU, BUT YOU ARE TO SEEK ME IN ANOTHER TIME AWAY. WHEN OUR SPIRITS ARE TOGETHER, WE'RE TOGETHER IN THE TRENCHES."

He explained to John that when he used the word volitional, he meant a conscious drawing apart, that it was a determination to turn his back on the world for a time. John told Jesus this was very enigmatic to him; he felt he was going from the real to the unreal when it ought to be the other way around.

"BE FLEXIBLE AND YIELD."

That made John feel ashamed. Jesus was pointing out that John had always put limits on how much he would give up to Him. He made it clear to John that if there were any walls between them it would be the ones John put there.

All this time, Jesus had been holding John in His arms, trying to reassure him there was nothing to fear in His presence, nothing to fear in giving up to Him.

John's Sixth Session

John immediately started experiencing some of the physical feelings of birth. His head felt the way it did the first night, but now, he knew to ask Jesus to give him strength.

He started to re-experience his birth, but suddenly stopped. He couldn't do it. When it got to the point where he couldn't get his breath, he panicked.

"Jesus, I can't do this! It feels like I'm dying. Do I have to go through this experience to be healed?"
"THIS IS SOMETHING THAT HURT YOU A GREAT DEAL. IT HAS CAUSED YOU TO HOLD BACK AS YOU APPROACH LIFE WITH ME. THE FEAR OF THAT PAIN IS THE LINE YOU WON'T CROSS WITH ME."

John asked Jesus how he could ever get over the fear of that pain. Jesus was holding his hand. John came to the realization that the worst thing about his birth was the fact that it took so long for him to be delivered. He started trying to breathe before he got out and couldn't get his breath. He told Jesus he thought he could take the physical pain, but he couldn't handle not being able to breathe. He asked Jesus if He would take the responsibility for his breathing as he went through the experience. Jesus said He would.

With that assurance, John was able to move on through his traumatic birth, and it took less than a minute to experience all of it.

"JUST REMEMBER THAT THE THINGS THAT APPEAR TO BE THREATS AREN'T REALLY THREATS WHEN I AM THERE."

Now, they were walking together, with neither of them talking very much. Jesus told John that if he ever felt the need to go through this experience again, He would be with him, and would always take responsibility for his breathing.

John's Seventh Session

John immediately felt the presence of Jesus. He was beginning to feel sad. He asked Jesus to tell him why he was feeling sad.

"BECAUSE SOME PEOPLE HAVE LEFT HIM AND HE'S FEELING REJECTED."

Jesus was talking about John's son. John asked Jesus if He would take away the boy's feelings of rejection.

When Jesus walked over and took the boy in His arms, he stopped crying. When Jesus put him down, the boy ran up to his room and started stuffing toys in a bag. The bag appeared to be bottomless because he put things in there from all around the room. Jesus asked him what he was doing. The boy told Him he was getting some stuff to take with him. Jesus told him he didn't need to take anything with him. And the boy replied, "But, I don't want to be all alone!"

Jesus was sitting on the side of the boy's bed.

"FOR THE TRIP YOU HAVE TO MAKE, THIS STUFF WILL JUST GET IN THE WAY."

Jesus took the boy in His arms and walked out the door. Outside, there was a winding staircase. Jesus started up the staircase, still carrying the boy. At some point, the staircase ended, but Jesus continued on without the benefit of stairs. All this time, John had been right behind them, but he couldn't go any higher than the top of the stairs. He was very sad there. After awhile, he started back down the stairs. It was a long way down. He could see the tops of trees and fields. When he finally got to the bottom, Jesus was there by himself. John asked where the boy was. Jesus just held out His arms to him. John was weeping now, very sad. Jesus started giving him assurance about his son.

"WHEN I CAME TO YOUR SON, HIS LIFE WAS INSECURE AND HE FELT REJECTED. I COMFORTED HIM AND HE ACCEPTED ME. WHEN I OFFERED HIM A CHANCE TO BE WITH ME, HE PUT ASIDE THE THINGS OF THE WORLD. WE BEGAN A WALK TOGETHER AND HE WAS TAKEN AWAY. JOHN, I WAS WITH YOU THROUGH ALL YOUR CRYING ABOUT THE LOSS OF YOUR SON, AND, IF IT HAD BEEN TOO MUCH FOR YOU TO HANDLE, I WOULD HAVE BEEN WILLING TO TAKE IT ON ME. YOU NEED TO GO AHEAD AND FEEL THE GRIEF. FEELING IT WON'T HARM YOU, BUT

NOT FEELING IT MIGHT. AS YOU DRAW NEARER TO ME, YOU WILL UNDERSTAND WHAT HAPPENED BETWEEN YOUR SON AND ME AND REALIZE THE IMPORTANCE OF IT. THERE IS NO WAY TO SUBLIMATE THE GRIEF."
"Jesus, with all the assurance and with all the understanding, I am still sad."

All this time they had been standing at the base of the staircase. Jesus told him that he had to invite others into his grief, that he must share it, and to remember that He was always holding John's hand.

At this point, Jesus left, heading back up the staircase.

This ended John's sessions. Except for the first few questions, and a few other questions I asked John for clarification, I had little part in the healing process except to be there and to take notes about what was transpiring. Jesus and the Holy Spirit were completely in charge. Although, compared to Primal Integration Therapy, this had been a quick healing, I had no assurance at that point that the process would work with other people. Later, I found having people turn directly to God for direction and healing works with almost everyone.

When John returned home, he was a different person. Friends were amazed at the change in him. Many came right out and asked what had happened to him. Because of his dramatic change, many others came for therapy. It has now been almost 20 years since John and I shared this beautiful healing by Jesus. His depression has surfaced from time to time over these years, but never lasts for any significant amount of time. Through this healing, Jesus gave him a new heart. Over the years, he has been a positive influence on the many lives he has touched. I know this to be true because of the positive influence he has been on my own life.

8.

Things the Holy Spirit taught me in working with John

⊹⇛⇚⊹

A s I've already mentioned, all I've learned about coun-seling with the Holy Spirit has come from being open to His direction and teaching. It seems I've been taught something in almost every counseling session, either as a revelation, or a confirmation of something already revealed. John was the first client I worked with where God was *directly* involved in the healing process, and there were a number of things learned in working with him. Here are some of the things the Holy Spirit taught me in my work with John.

1. God desires two-way communication with us

Probably the most important thing learned in working with John is God's wanting people to know of His desire to have a two-way communication with them and through this communication, to develop a personal relationship which would not otherwise exist. It seems the most important thing we offer clients is the opportunity to get used to asking God hard questions, learning to really listen and to distinguish God's voice.

2. God wants to be directly involved in the healing process

God wants to be directly involved in the healing process through the working of the Holy Spirit. God knows everything about us- even more than we know about ourselves. He knows things which have come down through our families, from ancestral bonds to values, all the negatives and the positives, and He knows everything that has ever happened to us. Who else has all the *facts* and who else knows exactly what we need in order to be healed? God is not limited in any way with the method used in order to bring healing to the individual. He provides the healing needed in the way that will be most acceptable to the individual. This was true with Jesus as He went about healing, and it hasn't changed with the times. With John, He used words, feelings, dreams, and visions. (I know of no other therapy dealing with *visions* of things that didn't actually happen to clients and God's messages in those visions.)

I learned with John that, as a counselor, the best thing I can do is stay out of the way of the working of the Holy Spirit. In John's sessions, my main job was to sit with John and take notes on a note pad. After the first day, I didn't even have to do anything to get him started. When he would close his eyes, Jesus would almost immediately come and minister to him. I believe God used those sessions with John to emphasize to me where the real healing comes from.

3. We have been given the power to bind Satan and negativity

We have the power to cause an evil spirit to leave by telling it to leave in the name of Jesus Christ. (The twisted little creature disappeared when John commanded it to leave in the name of Jesus.) We can cause Satan and any of his emissaries, as well as any negative feelings that Satan is using against us, to leave by binding and casting them out in the name of Jesus Christ. This is one of the great and effective weapons God places in our hands to deal with negative things which come into our lives. It's also a good way to confirm whether answers we get are truly coming from God.

4. Jesus was only crucified once

Some believers seem to feel we crucify Jesus every time we sin. Jesus made it very clear to John that just isn't true. In his healing John, Jesus told him, **"SEE, WHEN THE PAIN OF THE CROSS WAS OVER, IT WAS OVER."**
What He said is also an indication that, although there are some things we have to walk through in order to be healed, once the healing occurs, we don't have to keep dealing with the same thing over and over. One time and it's done. I have a good friend who had literally been all over the world seeking emotional healing. When I told him what we were doing here, he came down, planning to spend the week, having sessions every day. In the very first session, Jesus told him He had long since healed him and what he needed to do was to *acknowledge* that healing and accept it, and to stop looking for something he had already been given.

5. We tend to let our sins and unforgiveness come between us and God

Jesus pointed out to John that the reason he had not been walking with Jesus all the time was because he let two things come between them- the things he had done to others (his sins, which Jesus has forgiven if John has asked Him to) and the things others had done to him (his resentments and the reasons for the lack of forgiveness that was in him). Although Jesus' healings are fitted to the person and may not always have universal application, I believe this is one which might apply to many of us. I know it does to me. We are required to not only ask to be forgiven but also to forgive. In order to do this, we have to realize that forgiveness is an act of our *will* and not a feeling, and, once we ask Him to help us forgive whoever has hurt us, to take as fact that it is accomplished. If later, the thought of the person or the thing they did to us comes into our mind, we need to just acknowledge the thought and say, "That has already been dealt with," and it will go away.

We need to concentrate on Him and we can only do that when we have dealt with our own sins and with the hurts caused us by others. I think this ties in perfectly with the words of Jesus found in Matthew 5:23-24: "If you bring your gift to the altar and there remember that your brother has something against you, leave your gift before the altar and go be reconciled with your brother and then come back and offer your gift." This seems to make it crystal clear that we can't even worship God as we should until we get our earthly relationships straightened out.

6. Freedom means we can quit *doing*

Walking with Jesus is not complicated, although we sometimes try to make it so. We are a great deal like the Pharisees in that somewhere deep within us is a strong feeling we need to be *doing* things in order to win His acceptance. Here is a great truth: *the most important thing we can do for Jesus is to seek to become the person He originally created us to be.* In order to do that, we have to deal with our sins and with our resentments toward others. Once we do that, we are on the way to becoming the person He created us to be. At that point, all we need to do is put our arm around His shoulder and walk with Him. He is God, but He is also our brother. As our brother, He wants to guide us so our lives will be filled with peace, joy, and comfort in the Holy Spirit.

7. Jesus protects us when we are walking with Him

When we are walking closely with Jesus, nothing can touch us. It's like perfect peace- that indescribable state where nothing anyone does to us can touch our souls- our real being. This does not mean that bad things won't happen to us. They may or may not, but in this state, no matter what happens, our inner being, our soul, is intact and cannot be moved. Even when we walk closely with Jesus, there will continue to be things which hurt us, but His power is always there to protect us *if we call on Him.*

When we walk through situations to get to Jesus, things which may normally threaten us are no longer threats to us. This is a *mindset* which enables us to try things He suggests to us with a courage which can only come from Him, and without which, we would be too fearful to ever try.

8. He wants us to walk *through* our problems with Him

Somewhere, in growing up in the church, I got the impression that if I just had the right faith, I could pray to Jesus to remove problems from my life, and it would be done. In his dealing with John's problem, Jesus demonstrated He doesn't want to *remove* problems from our lives. He wants to teach us how to walk through them. In walking through them, we can learn a vital lesson we can use in helping others who are going through a similar kind of problem.

9. Our children are our commission

He emphasized to John that our children are our commission from God. This indicates that nothing is more important than our being good parents to our children. In addition, we need to realize they are only ours for awhile, so we need to make the most of the time we have with them. If there is anyone we need to encourage, it is these who are special gifts to us.

10. God wants us to be a reed, not a rock

Most of us, like John, need to learn to be more like a reed. We need to be open and flexible and not allow our beliefs to harden us to the point the world will wear us down. Remember what He told John: **"BE FLEXIBLE AND YIELD."**

11. We have to give control to Jesus

In order to come to Jesus, we have to give up control and, like the reed, just *be*. This, again, goes back to seeking to be the person God originally created us to be. A good prayer along these lines is to ask God to reveal the person He created you to be and to help you become that person.

Sometimes, we can get an indication as to who we were created to be by asking God if He has a special name for us. That name will usually give us an indication of what we started out being. There was a thought among early church fathers that salvation meant returning to the original creation, and not just a promise of heaven, being forgiven for our sins, or even a closer walk with God, although all of those things are true. Salvation is really a returning to being the person we were originally created to be.

12. We are not to try to fit Jesus into the world

We should not try to fit ourselves or Jesus into the world as we know it. I believe one of the biggest problems the church faces today is the tendency to do this. An example is the current practice by some authors of using the abbreviation "B.C.E." standing for "before the *common* era" instead of "B.C." standing for "before Christ." And, in place of using "A.D." for anno Domini, "in the year of our Lord," "C.E" standing for "*common* era" is used. In addition, many of the words of the great old hymns of the church have been changed to make them "politically correct" and inclusive. I have no problem with using inclusive wording in songs, but if that is desired, *new songs* should be written. Leave the old hymns as they were originally written! I refuse to accept the new wording of the hymns in our church, and you will hear me singing the old words if you are standing close by me. Some churches are reported to even be seeking new, more inclusive wording for "Father, Son, and Holy Spirit." Every time we do things like this, we are attempting to fit Jesus and Christianity into the world, and that is *exactly* what He says we are not to do.

13. Jesus has a place of peace and preparation for us

There is an invisible part of our realm that we cannot enter apart from Jesus. It is a place of preparation. In this place, we can draw close to wisdom and to strength. He told John we must separate the spirit and the physical. We need to *seek* that apartness. This was a revelation to me, and Jesus has given this same message to a number of people with whom we have worked. Several are noted in the other case histories.

14. The source of depression

Do you want a good explanation as to where depression comes from? Jesus told John his depression came from the world and from not keeping his thoughts on Jesus. Although

I've read a great deal on the subject and know depression can come from a number of things- like the loss of something that is held dear- it seems to ring true that *ultimately,* depression comes down to not focusing on *Him.*

15. We have too many pre-conceived ideas

We bring too many preconceived ideas with us into our Christian experience. This is confirmed in several of the other case histories. This is a strong indication that we need to question all of our beliefs- are they real, or are they something we have just accepted because it seemed everyone else believed them?

16. Jesus will always take on what we can't handle

When we are seeking healing, Jesus will always take on Himself anything that is too scary or painful for us to handle *if we will just ask Him.* He is always ready and willing, but He won't step in unless He is invited.

9.

Do You Want to be Healed?

In the fifth Chapter of the book of John is the story of a large group of blind and crippled people lying beside a pool called Bethesda in Jerusalem. They were waiting for an angel to come down and stir the water of the pool. They believed that, when this occurred, the first person in the pool was healed. One of the men there had had an infirmity for 38 years. When Jesus saw him there and knew he had been there for a long time, He said, "Wilt thou be made whole?" That's the King James interpretation of what He said. In words common today, it would be, "Do you want to be healed?" In the Bible, Jesus asked a number of people if they wanted to be healed before healing them.

I think Jesus knew that, unless a person truly *wants* to be healed, to be made whole, He could not heal them.

Why would a person *not* want to be made whole? There are a number of reasons. In thinking about this, I'm reminded of an essay that Ralph Waldo Emerson wrote on "Compensation." One of the points he made was that there are a finite number of things any of us can take on, so every time we take on something new, we give up something, generally our peace of mind. Basically the reason we don't

want to be healed is because there is something we don't
want to exchange for being healed. It may be the comfort or
the familiarity of the rut we are in as opposed to the unknown
condition which comes about with change. And, then, sometimes it's simply the fear of change itself.

Not long after working with John, I was approached by a
lady who asked if I would work with her daughter, who had
been diagnosed as schizophrenic. When I said I'd be glad to
see what I might be able to do for her, she said she would
bring the daughter to see me. As I was in prayer about their
visit, God spoke clearly to me,

"BEFORE YOU START WORKING WITH HER, ASK HER IF SHE *WANTS* TO BE HEALED.

When they arrived, I told the daughter that before we
did anything else, I needed to ask if she *wanted* to be healed.
She looked me straight in the eye and said, "Do you want an
honest answer?" I told her I did. She said, "Then the answer
is, "No."

At that, her mother exploded, "What do you mean you
don't want to be healed? Think of all the money we have
spent trying to help you! And, all the time it has taken to try
to take care of you, and all the emotional anguish you have
put us through!"

The daughter responded, "You asked me for an *honest*
answer and that's what I gave you. I may not like the rut I'm
in, but it's comfortable, and I have no responsibilities. I can
spend my days doing exactly what I want to do. If I were
to be healed, I would have to take on responsibilities that I
don't presently have, and don't want."

Needless to say, I could be of no help to this person, or to
anyone else who doesn't *want* to be healed.

I came away from this experience praising God for
His guidance. If I had not asked that key question, and had

attempted to try to be of help to her, there would have been no healing and I would have taken on a load of guilt, thinking there might have been something I should have done, but didn't. After this experience, whenever I question whether a person really wants to be healed, I come right out and ask the question, "Do you want to be healed?"

A second thing that came out of this experience is our policy of never allowing one person make an appointment for someone else. If someone asks us to work with another person, I tell them to ask *that* person to call to set up an appointment. You would be amazed at how many people want us to "fix" someone else- usually a husband, or wife.

Jesus, Himself, came right out and asked one of our clients if he wanted to be healed. This young man came from several hundred miles away. He had been on cocaine and had been arrested for dealing in cocaine. He did not profess to being a Christian, yet God spoke to him in words and visions. Early in the session, we had him ask, "God, do I need healing?" The answer he got was, **"YOU CERTAINLY DO!"** The next question was, "Do You want to heal me?"

After a few minutes, he said God was asking him a question. God said, **"DO YOU WANT TO BE HEALED?"** We asked him his answer to God's question. He said he wasn't sure, so we had him ask,

"Lord, what will it take for me to be healed?"
"YOU HAVE TO MAKE A CHOICE. YOU MUST CHOOSE BETWEEN COCAINE AND ME. YOU CAN'T HAVE BOTH."

We asked if he was ready to make a choice. He said he wasn't certain because, if he chose God, he was afraid he would lose all his friends. We had him ask God if that was so. After a minute or two, he started laughing. We asked what was happening. He said God told him the people he had been spending time with were not friends.

At that point, we had him ask, "Lord what will happen if I decide to follow You?" The answer was that there would be a coming together of his family and a sense of fulfillment in his life. Then, we had him ask what would happen if he chose cocaine. He started describing a vision where he saw himself dead on his bathroom floor, being found by his four year old son.

We told him it would accomplish nothing to go further until he made the decision- either to follow God's guidance, or stick with cocaine. We asked if he was ready to make that decision. He said he was not ready just then, but wanted to go back home and think about it. We let him know that, if he chose God, he could come back and we would find what else he needed to do in order to be completely healed. He said he would probably be back the next day. He didn't return. Several weeks later, he called for an appointment and we set one up, but he was a "no-show." Since he lived some distance from us, and we had no way to follow up on him, we never learned the end of this story.

10.

Interpreting Dreams

We've discovered that many times, Jesus speaks to us through our dreams. Several of the case histories shared in this book deal with asking Jesus to provide the symbolism of the different items in dreams and then to sum up the message of the dream.

We ask clients to record any dreams they experience while in therapy and bring those notes to our next session. Because there is a strong tendency to forget dreams, we suggest to clients that a pad and pencil be placed on their night table and, just before they go to sleep, to ask God to awaken them when they dream just long enough to record the dream. We also ask that if possible they turn on a light to make the notes. Otherwise, they may not be able to decipher their notes made in the dark.

When clients bring the notes from a dream, we have them first ask Jesus if He has any message for them in the dream. If He does, we then list the various items of the dream on the left side of a sheet of paper and, one by one, ask Jesus to reveal what each item symbolizes.

In interpreting dreams, sometimes the message of the dream seems clear after Jesus reveals the symbolism of each of the items in the dream. At other times, the message remains clouded. Whether it is clear or not, we *always* ask Jesus to sum up His message to clients in one or two sentences.

Molly is a good example of how Jesus helps interpret dreams. She and her husband had been divorced for several years. Molly was a Christian and had prayed for her husband's salvation while they remained married, and continued to pray for him in the years following their divorce. Her husband, Fred, had never seemed to be affected by her prayers.

Fred was tragically killed, and Molly was having a hard time dealing with his death. After having a dream about Fred, she came to see if the dream had been from God, and if there was a message in the dream.

We first asked God if He had a message for Molly in the dream. He said He did. In the dream, the first person Molly saw was her brother. Then, she saw Fred's boss. Next, she saw the house Fred was living in when he died. The house had an old, wooden floor. There was a bed there. She saw herself cleaning off a table. She saw Fred's body on the bed. There was no one there to take care of him. She only saw his backside and his feet. Then she was brushing her teeth, and lastly, she had been working hard and no one cared.

We laid out the dream on a sheet of paper. First, we listed everything in the dream on the left side of the sheet. Then, we went through these one by one, asking Jesus what the symbolism was and noted that in the right hand column. These are the things in the dream and what Jesus said they symbolized.

DREAM	SYMBOLIZES
Her brother	**LOVE AND FAMILY**
Fred's boss	**THE SECURITY FRED HAD HAD**

The house	**REFUGE**
The old wooden floor	**THE HOUSE WAS JUST A PLACE- NO LUXURIES**
The bed	**A PLACE OF REST**
Molly's cleaning off a table	**MOLLY WAS ACTIVE AND WANTED THINGS TO BE RIGHT**
Seeing Fred's body on The bed	**FRED WAS AT REST. HE WAS NOW OUT OF THE WORLD. HE COULDN'T BE HARMED ANY MORE, NOR COULD HE HARM ANYONE ELSE**
Molly's brushing her teeth	**THE TIME SHE HAD ACCEPTED JESUS AND WAS WASHED CLEAN**
Working hard and no one cared	**A LIE OF SATAN. JESUS SAID, "MOLLY, THEY DID CARE."**

When we asked Jesus to sum up in one or two sentences the message He had for Molly in the dream, He said, **"GOD'S LOVE GOES BEYOND THE GRAVE AND YOU ARE TO STILL PRAY FOR HIM. THE YEARS OF PRAYING WERE THE HARD WORK, AND I'M USING IT."**

Molly asked God if He was saying she should pray for Fred every day from then on and He said, **"NO. I WILL GIVE YOU A PEACE."** When she asked if God would give her a peace when Fred was released, God smiled and said, **"YES."**

Jesus' interpretation of her dream gave Molly great peace and comfort at a tough time in her life.

What God told Molly seems to indicate that death may not be an ending as far as salvation is concerned. There is a similar message from God in Paul's story in the chapter on Ancestral Bonds.

11.

The Religious Spirit

Many of our clients have needed healing for a "religious spirit." A religious spirit is an attitude based on *doing* instead of *being*. A religious spirit can drive people to attempt things that God never equipped them for, or cause them to take on so much "Christian" work, they burn themselves out. And, because none of us can do any job well for which God has not equipped us, a religious spirit can bring on a lot of guilt. For instance, it's fairly easy to get new Christians to take on any job in the church that needs doing. If this "baby" Christian isn't gifted in that area, but takes on the job because he feels he "ought to," he is setting himself up to be frustrated and to fail, and, in failing, to feel guilty he didn't do a better job. In my early Christian experience, I was personally caught up in that cycle. Over the years, I've learned the things in the church for which I'm *not* gifted, and today, when I'm asked to fill a job involving any of those areas, I simply say, "I appreciate being asked, but I'm not gifted in that area." That one statement has saved me a lot of grief.

A term with which we are all familiar is the "Christian Religion." Because of what the Holy Spirit has taught me through my own search for truth and from counseling people who had been misled by the teachings of their church, the label "Christian Religion" has become a contradiction of terms. The two words are as different as night and day. They are total *opposites* of one another.

Religion is a man-made system of laws and regulations, and Christianity is simply a *relationship* with God through Jesus Christ and the Holy Spirit.

When Jesus was in His ministry here on earth, it was the most religious people of His day, the scribes and Pharisees, who were always trying to prove Him wrong and, in the end, had Him crucified by the Romans. The 23rd chapter of Matthew gives an indication of what Jesus thought about religion as seen in the lives of the religious people of His time.

Because of the experiences we've had with those suffering from a religious spirit, we can't emphasize strongly enough how this spirit can negatively affect people's lives. If you get nothing else out of this book, it's our prayer that you determine not to get caught up in religion, but seek to have a *personal relationship* with Jesus Christ. This difference in religion and True Christianity may seem a strange idea, so let me share with you some of these differences. We use the term "True Christianity" because so many people have a warped sense of what Christianity is. It's so simple that many, many people miss the mark.

One of the best definitions for Christianity I've ever heard came from Peter. He grew up in a terribly dysfunctional family. At some point in growing up, he had acquired the deep feeling he was a reject, and that he would never amount to anything, even though he had a good mind and could have been a good student if he had had even a little confidence in himself.

I had worked with Peter using Primal Integration Therapy prior to the time we started having people talk with God. When I told him what we were currently doing, he said he wanted nothing to do with *anything* having to do with God or religion.

He shared with me that when he was young, his father, who believed in the literal translation of the Bible, *made* him go to church. If he didn't go, he was beaten. When he got into his teens and was big enough to defend himself against his father, he never darkened the doors of a church again. Because of his early experiences, he saw religion as bad, restrictive, and evil.

In the past, when he had come, we didn't seem to make much progress. I figured the only reason he had come back was that he was desperate and didn't know anyplace else to turn.

I explained that getting God into the healing process was much faster and much more effective than what I had previously done. I told him it probably wouldn't work with him, but I would appreciate his humoring me by at least giving it a try. Reluctantly, he said he would.

We started by having him ask some simple questions of Jesus like, "Lord, do You love me?" and "Is it Your will that I be here today?" At that point, he was lying on a mat with his eyes closed. After another question or two, all of a sudden, he opened his eyes, sat up on the mat and said, "Do you know the word I hate more than any other word in the world?" I said, "No. What word are you thinking of?" He said, "Christianity! I hate that word!" I said, "Is that right? Why don't you ask Jesus what the word Christianity means to Him."

He asked the question and after a few minutes, he had the answer, and it is one of the best definitions of Christianity I have ever heard. It could only have been straight from Jesus, because in his mind-set, Peter would have never come up with it. Peter said, **"He says that Christianity is my letting Him love me."**

It's so simple, and yet we try to complicate Christianity by getting it mixed up with religion.

Religious people do things out of a sense of duty, fear, or guilt. True Christians do things out of love and appreciation. True Christianity wants us to relax and just *be*, while religion tells us to labor and *do*. Religion puts burdens on us; True Christianity takes *our* burdens and gives us lighter burdens. Religion wants us to conform, to all be alike; True Christianity wants each of us to be the unique person God originally created us to be. Religion is trying to make our way up to God through our works; True Christianity is gratefully accepting His free gift. Religion brings obligation, guilt, and anxiety. True Christianity brings peace, joy, and fulfillment.

Religion complicates things and puts more of a burden on us than God ever intended for us to carry. True Christianity simplifies things if we will just let it. A good example of this is the story of Bill's healing from a religious spirit.

When Bill came to us back in the early 90's, he had a serious stress- related illness. As we talked with him, we learned that he had a rough time as a youngster, having grown up in a dysfunctional home.

He felt the call of God to the ministry relatively early in his life, and had been serving churches in his area of the country for a number of years. He was a good preacher, and an even better minister. He cared deeply for his congregations, to a fault. He took the problems of others on himself and literally got under their load. In addition, he was a perfectionist as far as his church was concerned, and was involved in every aspect of the work of his church.

Bill turned out to be one of those fortunate ones to whom Jesus brought healing in several ways- in words, in feelings, in visions, and in dreams. Right off the bat, Jesus told Bill he had needed healing since his childhood. He said Bill had a problem with self-esteem.

When Bill asked Jesus to show him how *He* saw his situation, Bill saw himself in a pressure cooker. When he asked Jesus if the pressure cooker had a name, He said,

"**SALVATION BY WORKS.**" Jesus said salvation by works was a problem for Bill because He had learned to *get* acceptance by his works. Jesus said He wanted to heal him of this, and he could be healed by relaxation. He defined relaxation as being at peace with himself and in his relationships with other people.

Bill asked some other questions and got no answers. He asked Jesus why He wasn't answering. Jesus said there was a barrier between them that kept Bill from hearing. The name of the barrier was *conditioning*. Jesus said conditioning controlled Bill's first response. Bill asked Jesus if He would remove this conditioning from him. Jesus said that He would *in time*. He said it would take time because Bill had to unlearn some old behaviors. He told him the first thing he would have to unlearn was that he needed to *earn* people's approval, and he could learn that by trusting Jesus.

Bill asked if any of the problems he was currently experiencing had come down through his family. Jesus replied that a feeling of unworthiness had come down through his mother's side going back three generations, to his grandparents. Some mental illness in the family had given the family a feeling of unworthiness. Jesus said He was healing his family of that bond as they talked.

Jesus said He knew Bill was going through a hard time, but he shouldn't think about giving up. Bill needed to come up with a division of labor in his church, letting some of the members take responsibility for some of the things he had been doing. Jesus ended that session by saying,

"I'M ALLOWING YOU TO GO THROUGH THIS TO MAKE YOU OF GREATER USEFULNESS. DON'T RESENT THE PROCESS."

In our second session, Jesus indicated He wanted to deal with the resentment Bill had been carrying toward his mother.

He said Bill could be healed of this by not making any more excuses for his mother, by accepting the fact that she had problems, and that she hurt him. Bill started confessing this to Jesus. He said, "Lord, my mother *did* hurt me. She hurt me physically. She embarrassed me. Many nights she kept me awake with all her rambling around. She made me fearful. She made me into someone I wasn't." When he asked Jesus if that covered it, Jesus said, **"AT TIMES YOU HATED HER."** Bill said, "Lord, I *was* angry with her. I still am. What can I do to get rid of the anger I feel toward mother?" Bill started seeing cool-looking colors- green and blue. Jesus told him this was symbolic of *His* peace. He said, **"YOU NEED TO COME TO TERMS WITH THIS ANGER AND BE AT PEACE WITH YOUR MOTHER."** When Bill asked how he could do that, Jesus said, **"YOU HAVE ALREADY CONFESSED IT. NOW, QUIT USING IT TO FEEL SORRY FOR YOURSELF."**

Jesus said it would be helpful for Bill to know *why* his mother was the way she was. In his mind, Bill saw a turbulence of some kind. Jesus said his mother's home life was abusive, and that her daddy was abusive. Bill asked if there was anything about his being born that caused a problem for his mother, because he had felt guilty about the fact that he may have made her life worse when he was born. There was no answer, but suddenly, Bill said he felt suspended between his chair and the ceiling of the room, just a gentle undulation of his body gently flowing. Jesus said this was freshness and symbolized cleaning. He said he was taking Bill through a healing. Bill asked if there was anything else Jesus wanted to tell him about his mother. He said Bill should have compassion for his mother and he needed to forgive her. Bill asked how he could do that; could he just say, "I forgive her?" In his mind, he saw a cemetery. He asked if he should go to her grave and tell her he forgave her. Jesus said he could, and while he was there, he should also forgive his father.

He said they both did the best they knew how. Bill said he was feeling some pain because he had not told his mother he forgave her while she was living. He said, "Lord, if I go out to their graves and tell them I forgive them, will they somehow know that?" Jesus said that when Bill did this, a healing would occur.

In our next session, Bill asked why he was feeling so depressed. Jesus told him it was because he had lost something. In his mind, Bill saw a man on crutches and asked if that was him. Jesus said it was. He asked if he still needed the crutches. Jesus told him he could cast them away. Bill asked the name of the crutches and Jesus said **"EXCUSES-EXCUSES FOR NOT BEING WHOLE. EXCUSES HAVE GOTTEN YOU ATTENTION."** Bill said, "Do I *need* excuses to get attention?" Jesus said he didn't need them anymore; people would love him for what he was, and not because of what had happened to him.

Bill saw an image of an old army fort with massive gates that just opened. Jesus said this meant he could walk out into freedom. Bill got a clear image of himself walking out. The fort was dingy and dirty. Outside, it was beautiful.

Jesus said if he would continue to walk in this freedom, the stress that had caused his physical problems would lessen. Jesus said he also needed to take time for himself; he should exercise, he should delegate some of his church work and he should relax in the work. Bill said, "If I relax and take time for myself, how will things get done?" Jesus said there were people there to help him. He said, **"YOU DON'T NEED THE PRAISE YOU GET FOR BEING OVERWORKED."**

In our next session, Jesus said He wanted to talk to Bill about the fact he hadn't slept well the night before. He said the reason was Bill's conditioning. He said it was *normal* for Bill to not sleep well. Bill saw himself back in his home. He was going from room to room following his mother. She had a cigarette in her hand and she was stumbling around. He heard her calling him all during the night. He couldn't go to sleep because he was afraid she might fall and he wouldn't hear her. Jesus said he still listened for things when he went to bed. When Bill asked Jesus if He wanted to heal him of the conditioning, he saw a wall and two people doing a tug of war with a rope. Jesus said this was symbolic of Satan not wanting him healed. Bill asked if he could bind the wall and cast it out in Jesus' name, and when he got a **"YES,"** he did. He asked Jesus if there was anything else he needed to do. Jesus said, **"SAY GOOD-NIGHT TO MOTHER."** He said Bill needed to do that every night when he went to bed, and he would have a good night's sleep. He said Bill also needed to forgive her for keeping him awake. Bill told his mother he forgave her for all those awful nights when he had been so terrified. At that point, he saw a clock on the wall and Jesus told him it signified a process of healing *in time.*

Bill saw a door that was closing, and he felt the suspension he had felt the first day. He asked Jesus what was happening, and Jesus said He was carrying him because He loved him. Bill said, "Jesus, I feel something like heat leaving my body. What is that?" Jesus said it was a cleansing. Then he saw fire racing across the stubble of a wheat field, consuming it. Jesus said He was taking away things Bill did not need. Then he saw sprigs of green grass beginning to come up from the charred ground and Jesus said it was new life and growth and physical, emotional, and spiritual health.

When Bill came the next day, he remembered a dream from the night before. Jesus indicated He had a message to him in the dream. In the dream, Bill and his wife were traveling by taxi to an airport. When they arrived at the airport, they got their suitcases out but left some clothes on hangers in the cab. Bill frantically searched for them. In frustration, he resigned himself to the fact they were lost. Then he realized he could just get new ones, and was at peace as they left on their journey.

We asked Jesus to interpret the dream for him. Their being in a taxi on the way to the airport symbolized getting away. The hanging clothes left in the taxi symbolized things that were not needed. The frantic searching for the clothes symbolized a loss of security. Frustration and the fact the clothes were lost symbolized the way Bill had been living. Resigning himself to the fact they were lost symbolized his finally being willing to give the clothes up. Realizing that he could get new ones symbolized newness and growth, a fresh start. Calmness and peace symbolized there were parts of Bill he could leave and move on without.

We then asked Jesus to sum up in one or two sentences specifically what His message was.

"IT IS FEARFUL TO CHANGE OLD WAYS OF LIFE, BUT AS THEY ARE LEFT, PEACE COMES AND THE JOURNEY IS FUN."

Bill said at this point, he saw a lush green field that was flourishing.

Finally, Jesus said he wanted to say something about Bill's work. He said Bill had been running frantically just like he did at the airport, and that he had been carrying baggage that would be o.k. to lose. When Bill asked how he would know what to keep and what to let go, Jesus said he should stay close to Him and ask Him.

In our next session, Bill asked Jesus why he became depressed over the week-end.

"GRIEF."
"Lord, would You define "grief?"
"THE LOSS OF SOMEONE DEAR. YOU ARE GRIEVING OVER A LITTLE BOY."

"Lord, is the little boy gone?"
"HE IS GOING AWAY."
"Was this *my* little boy?'
"IT WAS AND YOU DON'T NEED HIM ANY MORE."
"Lord, is he going away, or am I going to have a healed little boy?"
"IT WILL BE A DIFFERENT LITTLE BOY AND HE WILL BE A SOURCE OF HEALING."

Because the little boy had been a source of pain, Bill had wanted him to leave. The little boy wouldn't be a source of pain anymore. Jesus said the little boy would be a source of *pleasure* if Bill would make him his friend. When Bill asked how he could do that, he saw a baseball diamond with players warming up. He asked Jesus if He was saying he needed practice loving the little boy. **"YES."**

Bill started visualizing a train. At first, he was the engineer. Then he left and walked back to a car with a comfortable seat and sat down. He asked Jesus if He was showing him that He wanted him to leave the driving to Him.

"YES, AND I WANT YOU TO ENJOY THE RIDE."

At that point, the train was moving through a lush countryside, then through a resort area, and finally onto the side of a mountain with nothing below him. Jesus said this symbolized trust, that He was telling Bill to trust in Him and let Him move him on out.

There was exercise equipment in the car where Bill was sitting. That meant he should take care of himself physically, that he should get on an exercise program.

Before we started our next session, Bill told me about a tree next to his house that he needed to take down, but taking it down would mean having to climb up in the tree and cut it off from the top so as not to damage his home. He had a rope, a saw and a ladder, but he was afraid to climb up in the tree. On the other hand, he was afraid to *not* climb up there and get the job done. When we started the conversation with Jesus, He said the tree symbolized Bill's limitations; that every time Bill saw the tree it reminded him of what he *couldn't do*. When he asked Jesus what He wanted to tell him about his limitations, he saw himself hugging the tree.

"EMBRACE THE LIMITATIONS."

When he asked Jesus how he could do that, he saw a hammock strung between two trees and he was resting in it. Jesus said that meant he was to be at peace with those limitations, that it was alright to relax with them. Jesus went on to say that Bill had been fighting his limitations and that was creating pressure on him. He needed to learn to back away.

As our final session started, Bill felt that warm, light feeling and saw the most pleasant, visible air waves, flowing gently, rich blue and green strands, gentle and calm. There seemed to be a rhythm within him of those gentle waves. Jesus said this symbolized peace, finding relief from the burdens he had been carrying, and it had to do with Bill's coming to peace about embracing his inadequacies and peace about himself. Bill saw a man in a superman outfit, but he was old and wrinkled. He wasn't what Superman was supposed to look like. Jesus told him this symbolized that there were other ways to be strong. Bill could see the heart of that superman pounding, almost growing larger, and Jesus said that symbolized inner strength.

When Bill asked how he could use that knowledge to gain peace about himself and about what was going on, he had a vision of himself with his arms around that tree again.

"Lord, are You saying that in order to gain peace within myself and with other's needs, I just need to embrace my inadequacies

"YOUR HEAVENLY FATHER SEES THE NEEDS OF THE BIRDS, AND HE WILL CARE FOR YOU AND SEE TO YOUR NEEDS TOO."

"Lord, are You saying I need to do what I can, but realize You have the final responsibility?" (He got that light feeling again.)

"YES."

"How do I turn this responsibility over to You?"

He saw himself reclining, wearing a pair of stereo head-phones. Jesus said this meant he needed to be still, to relax and listen.

Bill said he was now at the end of a conveyor belt with an endless stream of roses passing just under his nose. When he asked what that symbolized, he saw Jesus laughing. It was so obvious. **"RELAX AND SMELL THE ROSES."** Bill felt he was floating. The image of Jesus was getting smaller and he could hear His laughter fading off in the distance, as He went out of sight.

Today, Bill continues to have a very active ministry but finds time to relax and smell the roses, and he has also become a friend to his little boy. He is in good health physically. In speaking with Bill later about his experiences in therapy, he told me over the years, he had been to a number of therapists, but it was only in these sessions where he was talking with Jesus that he experienced visions.

Getting back to our thoughts on religion, religion tends to want to give "cookie cutter, one-size-fits-all" solutions to problems. True Christianity gives *individual* solutions tailored to the situation and to the person asking God for help.

Lucy's healing is a good example of what we mean by "cookie cutter, one-size-fits-all solutions." Initially, it was hard for her to receive healing because of preconceived concepts she had been taught, or had caught in her church. Lucy is one of those we could not contact because we've lost track of her. We've changed enough of her story so that only she should be able to know it's hers.

Lucy's husband had been emotionally and physically abusive for most of their married life. She had stayed with him for almost 20 years, until their children were grown. At that point, she separated from him, but didn't even consider a divorce because her church did not sanction divorce.

When she came, she was complaining about a backache. Here is her conversation with Jesus:

"Jesus, do You want to heal me?"
"YES."
"What will it take in order for me to be healed?"
"I CAN'T TELL YOU."
"What do You mean, You can't tell me?"
"BECAUSE YOU WON'T BELIEVE ME."

(At that point, we stopped and discussed what that might mean. We asked if she was willing to be open to *whatever* he might tell her. She finally said she would do her best to keep an open mind.)

"Lord, I want to be open to whatever You want to tell me. Would You please tell me what it will take for me to be healed?"
"YOU NEED TO GO HOME AND DIVORCE YOUR HUSBAND. YOU CAN NEVER BECOME THE PERSON I CREATED YOU TO BE IN THAT KIND OF ABUSIVE RELATIONSHIP."

The idea of God's being against divorce had been so strongly programmed into Lucy, she questioned if this had really come from God. She returned home and talked with the elders of her church about what she felt she had received from God. Typically, she was told she needed to return to her husband and just be a submissive wife and that would take care of the situation.

This is what we call a "cookie cutter, one-size-fits-all" solution. Now she was in a quandary. She had tried to be open so she could hear God's directions for her. She had taken the issue to the church elders, which was what she had been taught to do. I believe it was because she had made such an effort to do the *right* thing that the Holy Spirit stepped in and started working on her husband. I got a call from her telling me that before she could come to a conclusion about what she should do, her husband divorced *her*. She felt that a large load had been lifted from her back and she was set free. It's no wonder she had a backache when she had come.

About ten years later, we received another call from this lady telling us she is now a counselor in her area, helping hurting people who are going through rough times, like she did. It's obvious Satan used the religious people in her church to try to mislead her and prevent her from becoming a counselor. If she had taken the counsel of the elders of her church, she would have gone back into an abusive situation and would undoubtedly have been miserable the rest of her life, instead of being in a place of great service, joy and fulfillment.

Since we are on the subject of divorce, we want to share with you something another lady experienced when she talked with Jesus, which sheds a little more light on God's feeling about divorce.

This lady was also a committed Christian. Her husband had broken their relationship and had separated from her.

She had been devastated by what he had done. She came looking for answers about what she should do concerning their marriage. Like others we'd worked with, she had the preconceived belief that once married, always married; divorce was not an option.

In the course of many sessions about what she should do, God pointed out that, in His eyes, a divorce occurs anytime one of the two fails to live up to the *commitment* they made when they married. Her husband had broken his commitment when he failed to love her, comfort her, honor and keep her. God told her that going to court to get a document of divorcement was simply an *acknowledgement* of what had already occurred.

I know God is opposed to divorce because He is opposed to anyone failing to live up to a commitment made. Although he is opposed to divorce, He seems to be more opposed to two people continuing to be husband and wife in name only. That is hypocrisy, and he hates hypocrisy.

While we are on the subject of religion, we think this is the place to tell you about Jerry's conversation with Jesus about the United Methodist Church. While this conversation is specifically about the United Methodist Church, we believe what Jesus had to say can be applied to almost any universal church.

Jerry was an active member of the United Methodist Church in his city. Over the years he had been on the Official Board and had headed up several committees. There were some things that concerned him about his church, so he questioned Jesus about it.

When Jerry asked Jesus if he wanted to tell him anything about the church, Jesus said He wanted to show Jerry the *pride and the arrogance* of the United Methodist Church. He said while there was no hope for the church *as a major force*, there was rising up a group of people who love Jesus more than they love the church, and that would compose His true church.

"Lord, is there any church where people should go?"
"VARIOUS CHURCHES SERVE VARIOUS NEEDS. THERE WILL NEVER BE A MANMADE CHURCH THAT WILL MEET ALL THESE NEEDS. NEW WINE WILL ALWAYS DEMAND NEW WINESKINS.

Jesus went on to say that churches should be established on *needs*; the first of these needs being the need for salvation. Then, churches should be established on those who will be open and honest enough to see the needs people have and minister to those needs.

"Are You saying everyone in the church should be a minister?"
"YES. THAT HAS ALWAYS BEEN THE WAY IT WAS INTENDED, BUT THE SIN OF THE CHURCH TODAY IS THAT THEY PAY A MINISTER TO MINISTER FOR THEM."
"How have we have missed the mark so far?"
"BY REFUSING TO BE PEOPLE OF THE BOOK, BY VALUING MEN'S OPINIONS MORE THAN MY WORD, AND BY SPIRITUAL SLOTH."

Jesus continued talking about the church. He said He was seeing a leprous body, full of scabs, sores, and runny eyes. In His eyes, this is the church of today. He said there was very little life left in the church, but enough life that all could still be changed. He said the church started dying when it rejected the Holiness Movement and the movement of His Spirit in 1900. He said that, by and large, the church is full of hirelings and sheep stealers instead of shepherds who care for men's souls.

"THEY HAVE THEIR REWARDS, BUT NOT THE KINGDOM OF HEAVEN."

He said the church could be healed if faithful pastors would fearlessly declare His truth, but the standards by which we judge our church have to be changed. Jesus explained what He meant by that:

"THE CHURCH IS NOT A BUILDING, NOR IS IT A SOCIAL CLUB, NOR IS IT NAMES ON A LIST. THE CHURCH IS THE BODY OF CHRIST AND INDIVIDUAL MEMBERS OF HIM ARE THOSE WHO HAVE REPENTED AND BEEN BORN AGAIN. THE REASON THAT MOST CHURCH MEMBERS DO NOT SEE THE KINGDOM OF GOD IS THAT THEY HAVE NOT BEEN BORN AGAIN AND HAVE BEEN CONVERTED *TO THE CHURCH* AND NOT TO THE KINGDOM OF GOD. "TO BE BORN AGAIN IS TO BECOME ALIVE IN THE SPIRIT AND TO BE A NEW SPIRITUAL CREATURE IN WHICH OLD THINGS ARE PASSED AWAY AND IN WHICH THE NEW HAS COME. IT IS A GIFT FROM ME TO THOSE WHO LOOK TO ME FOR THEIR SALVATION AND ASK MY SON TO COME INTO THEIR LIVES."
"Is there any hope for the United Methodist Church?"
"YES. THERE IS HOPE, BUT IT DOES NOT LIE WITHIN THE BOUNDS AS IT IS PRESENTLY RECOGNIZED. THERE WILL BE POCKETS OF BELIEVERS IN VARIOUS

UNITED METHODIST CHURCHES THAT WILL REMAIN AS SALT AND LIGHT AND LEAVENING. OTHERS WILL BE CALLED TO A PLACE THAT I WILL SHOW THEM."

"Are You saying the United Methodist Church could be reworked?"

"WHEN THE WINE OF THE SPIRIT IS POURED, THERE MUST BE NEW WINESKINS. THE WINESKINS OF THE METHODIST CHURCH HAVE BECOME DRY AND BRITTLE. THE FERMENT OF NEW WINE WOULD BURST THE SKINS AT THE SEAMS."

"Is there anything else You want to tell me about the church?"

"BE ALERT TO THE MOVING OF THE SPIRIT. AS CHURCH PEOPLE, YOU SHOULD PRAY FOR THE PASTOR, THAT HE MIGHT BE BOLD. MAKE CERTAIN OF YOUR OWN SALVATION AND REALIZE FOR EVERY SPIRITUAL EXPERIENCE YOU HAVE, THERE IS MORE. COME TOGETHER WITH THOSE OF LIKE MINDS. STORM THE GATES OF HEAVEN. PRAY WITHOUT CEASING. BE A PRAISING PEOPLE."

Getting back to our general thoughts on Christianity and Religion, it's obvious that any manmade organization works more efficiently if the members of that organization are made to conform. Certainly, a business of 100 employees could not operate effectively if their people headed out in 100 different directions based on their own ideas and reasoning. Conformity is *required* for a business to be successful and, unfortunately, the church operates on the same concept, especially in the area of structure and leadership. True

Christianity does not seek conformity, but the freedom to be the unique person God created each of us to be.

"Religious" people in churches can be used by Satan to turn off people to True Christianity. I personally know people who have left the church because one of the "religious" people in their church complained whenever they didn't wear a coat to church, or didn't fit the mold in some other way.

One last thing about the religious spirit and this thing of "being" and "doing." We tend to get this backwards. We seem to think that if we will just do good works, we can become the person God wants us to be. The truth is, we first need to ask Him to help us become the person He created us to be and out of that journey will come what we can do for Him. When we get the *doing* ahead of the *being*, we are heading in the wrong direction. "Doing" is the world's way. "Being" is God's way.

12.

Satan

1 Peter 5:8: Be sober, be vigilant; because your adversary the devil, as a roaring lion, walketh about, seeking whom he may devour.

Ephesians 6:12: For we wrestle not against flesh and blood, but against principalities, against powers, against the rulers of the darkness of this world, against spiritual wickedness in high places.

Some writers tend to stay away from discussing much about Satan, feeling that discussing him gives place to him. I disagree. In this world, we are at war and, as Christians, our fight is against Satan. No General would think of going into battle without first learning all he can about his enemy. I think it's even more important that we become familiar with the way Satan operates, so that we can better resist him since our fight with him is not just a single battle, but a lifelong war.

Over the past 20 years, I've learned much more about Satan than I had ever known before, and one of the main things I've learned in dealing with him is that when Satan comes into a conversation or a situation with one of his lies, he can be bound and cast out in the name of Jesus Christ so that the truth can come through.

Satan can imitate the voice of God, and he seeks ways of coming into the conversation whenever we are talking with God. Satan can be very subtle. He has to be. If what he said was always stupid or out of place, it would be easy to tell when he chimes in. It's when there's a touch of truth in what he says that it becomes a problem. Once I had a lady talking with Jesus about her father, who had been abusive to her. When she asked if there was anything about her relationship with her daddy that she needed to look at, the answer she got was, "Your daddy was an ego-maniac who didn't care anything about you one way or the other." Since God almost never tells anyone something that negative about another person, I had a strong feeling the answer wasn't from God, so I had her say, "Satan, I bind you and cast you out in the name of Jesus Christ." Then, she asked, "Lord was he really an ego-maniac?" God said, **"NO. HE WAS MISGUIDED. HE KNEW WHAT I WANTED HIM TO DO, BUT HE WASN'T ABLE TO DO IT."** (We found just a little later that an ancestral bond which he was not aware of had him bound and caused him to be misguided.) I also recall a time when the answer a lady received *seemed* to be right on the money. When we had her ask God what she needed to do to get closer to God, the answer she got was that she needed to spend more time reading the Bible. I knew this lady, and knew she already spent a *lot* of time doing just that. Something about that answer just didn't ring true, so we had her say, "Satan, I bind you and cast you out in the name of Jesus Christ!" Then we asked the Lord if the answer had been from Him, and the answer was **"NO."**

We found Jesus' real answer to her question was, **"SPEND MORE TIME TALKING WITH ME."** Jesus wanted a closer relationship. Satan didn't want her to hear *that*, so he picked a *lesser* thing that he might convince her to do. Whenever Satan can't directly keep us from doing what God wants us to do, he does *anything* to buy time, hoping he can get us off track.

God has given us a great weapon to use against Satan-the power of Jesus Christ to bind him and cast him out. Matthew 16:19 explains..."whatsoever thou shalt bind on earth shall be bound in heaven; and whatsoever thou shalt loose on earth shall be loosed in heaven." James 4:7 tells us, "Resist the devil and he will flee from you." We resist him by binding and casting him out in the name of Jesus. Over time, we have learned that whenever we question the answer a client gets, we can check it out by having the client bind Satan and cast him out in the name of Jesus Christ. We then repeat the question and see if we get the same answer. If we do, it is a good indication the answer *was* from God.

If you are a Christian, any guilt you experience comes to you directly from Satan. Romans 8:1 tells us "There is therefore now *no condemnation* to them which are in Christ Jesus, who walk not after the flesh, but after the Spirit." When we ask Jesus to forgive us for our transgressions, He does just what we ask, and holds us guilty no longer. Therefore, if we feel guilt, and *He* isn't condemning us, the guilt is coming from Satan and is one of his lies. To get rid of the feeling of guilt, we need to consciously bind and cast Satan out in the name of Jesus Christ.

If you are a Christian and are abnormally fearful, that fear is coming from Satan. We are told in 2 Timothy 1:7, "For God has not given us the spirit of fear, but of power, and of love, and of a sound mind." Here again, when feelings of fear come, we can bind them and cast them out in Jesus' name.

If you are a Christian and feel insecure, that insecurity is coming from satan. In truth, there is no greater security than in having a relationship with Jesus. The feeling of insecurity is another of Satan's lies. We can deal with insecurity the same as we deal with guilt and fear.

If you are a Christian and you feel a lot of anger, that anger is coming from Satan. Ephesians 4:31states, "Let all bitterness, and wrath, and anger, and evil speaking be put away from you, with all malice." We can deal with anger the same as we do with the other negative feelings. The Bible also tells us to *be angry*, but sin not. "Let not the sun go down on your wrath" (Ephesians 4:26). God wants us to *acknowledge* our anger and ask Him to help us deal with it.

Many people who come for counseling are angry with *God* for one reason or another. Many times, they are not aware of the anger they have toward Him, because Satan is good at convincing people they *can't* be angry with God. When we feel this may be the case, we have the client ask God if it's okay to be angry with Him. The answer is always "YES." The truth is, God knows *everything*, so our owning up to the fact that we are angry with Him is really just acknowledging what He already knows. Once we acknowledge how we feel, He can help us deal with it.

Mike, a minister who was frustrated in the ministry and depressed when he came is a good example of a person being angry with God but not realizing he was carrying that anger.

God told Mike his frustration and depression came from his seeing his being a minister in a church a burden. He told Mike He had forgotten Mike's sins and had taken his burden. He said His yoke was easy, but that Mike saw the ministry as a *responsibility* and *a heavy burden*. Mike saw the ministry the way he did because of his perception, which was not real. Mike asked Jesus to define "real" for him. Jesus said real was what really is, not what Mike perceived it to be.

Jesus said He wanted to change Mike's perception. When Mike asked if Jesus *would* change it, Jesus said, "IF YOU ARE WILLING." He said the reason Mike might not be willing had to do with control. Mike asked Jesus to explain that.

"THERE ARE TIMES WHEN YOU DOUBT I WILL DO A GOOD JOB WITH IT."

Mike asked if his faith needed to be increased.

"NO. YOU BELIEVE. JUST BE TRUE. MUSTARD SEED."
"Lord, are you saying that I need to *will* to give the problems to You?"
"YES. YOU WANT TO, BUT YOU DON'T."
"How can I be sure I have given them to You?"
"FAITH."

Mike asked if God was bringing *counseling* into his ministry. Jesus told him he needed to grow, and this would be as much for his benefit as it would be for those who come to him. Mike felt some fear about this, and Jesus said that fear was coming from Satan, that Satan wanted to discourage him. Jesus said Mike's perception of himself was that he was not good enough to counsel, that he had worse problems than those who would be coming to him, and that he was not qualified. Jesus confirmed Mike *wasn't* qualified, but *He* was and Mike should point them to Him and He would counsel them through Mike.

In our second session, Jesus told Mike that when he was 24, the year his mother died, he had picked up a burden of anger that he had carried now for 23 years. He had picked up that burden because Jesus didn't control that situation. When Mike asked if he was mad at God, the answer was **"YES."** He asked if it was okay to be angry at God, and the answer was again **"YES."** Jesus said what had happened in the situation with his mother had caused Mike to mistrust and distrust.

"Lord, why didn't You answer my prayers and heal my mother?"

"I DID."

"Would You explain that?"

"SHE WAS HEALED." (Jesus was talking about the ultimate healing for everyone- death.)

"Jesus, she was the one who was happiest with my entering the ministry. She was the only one who was supportive and she died right after that. Why did You take away the one who was supportive of me?"

"I DIDN'T TAKE HER AWAY.

"Lord, would You please explain that?"

"YOU DIDN'T NEED HER FOR SUPPORT, EVEN THOUGH YOU PERCEIVED YOU DID. *I* WAS THE ONE WHO CALLED YOU."

Not knowing what he should ask next, Mike asked what his next question should be.

"WHY ARE YOU ANGRY WITH ME FOR TAKING YOUR MOTHER WHEN I DON'T TAKE MOTHERS, AND OTHER PEOPLE'S MOTHERS DIE JUST AS YOURS DID?"

"Lord, wouldn't You be upset if Your mother died?"

"POSSIBLY."

"Then, why do You ask me why I'm angry with You?"

"THE QUESTION WAS FOR YOUR BENEFIT."

"Lord, why *am* I angry?"

"BECAUSE YOU FELT BETRAYED. YOU FELT LET DOWN, NOT SUPPORTED. YOU THOUGHT YOU WERE DOING SOMETHING

FOR ME, AND I SHOULD HAVE REWARDED YOU. YOU THOUGHT YOU WERE PLEASING ME BY DOING SOMETHING EXTRA. BEING OBEDIENT WAS ONLY YOUR REASONABLE SERVICE."

Mike asked if he had prayed amiss when he asked for his mother to be healed. Jesus said he hadn't. Mike asked if Jesus wanted to heal him of his anger and Jesus said He did.

"Lord, what difference will it make if You heal me?"
"JOY AND PEACE. CONTENTMENT WHERE YOU ARE."
"What do I need to do to be healed?"
"COMPLETELY TRUST IN MY GOODNESS AND MY LOVE AND UNDERSTANDING YOUR HEART, THAT IT ISN'T FICKLE."

When he asked what it would take for him to completely trust, Jesus said, **"UNDERSTANDING, *HEART* UNDERSTANING."** Mike asked, "Lord has my healing already started?" **"IT IS DONE."** Mike said, "It's like I knew God called me and I was glad of it, but I couldn't back out because my mother was so pleased about it." He asked, "Lord, is that one of the places I picked up the feeling I had no choice about the ministry?" Jesus said, **"THAT IS *THE* PLACE."**

He asked Jesus if his mother had any idea what he had been going through. Jesus said she did. Then Mike asked, "Has she been praying I would come to the place where I would realize she didn't mean it like I've taken it?" Jesus said, **"YES. SHE WANTS YOU PEACEFUL AND CONTENT."** Jesus went on to confirm that there was rejoicing in heaven because He had been able to show this to Mike.

Mike said, "I didn't want to fail because I wanted mother to see me successful. Lord, does she see me as successful if I never do another lick, if I'm not in the ministry?" **"YES. SHE SEES SUCCESS WHERE SHE IS, WITH ME."** Mike asked Jesus to define "success,"

"COMPLETE TRUST IN ME. COMPLETE TRUST IN MY LOVE, TO RELAX IN IT."

Mike went back to talking about his mother's last days, asking Jesus if she was at the point she couldn't get well.

"ONE CAN ALWAYS GET WELL, BUT YOUR MOTHER WOULD NOT HAVE BEEN ABLE TO FUNCTION, AND SHE WOULD NOT HAVE BEEN WITHOUT PAIN."

When Mike asked if there could be healing and the person still be in pain, Jesus told him pain was a part of healing. Mike asked, "Jesus, did You tell me that a person can always get well?"

"YES. NOT ON EARTH. YOU MISUNDER-STOOD. YOUR MOTHER COULD NOT HAVE BEEN HEALED ON EARTH. SHE WAS AT THE POINT SHE COULDN'T GET WELL."

When our next session started, Jesus said He wanted to talk about freedom, and He defined freedom as complete trust. When Mike asked what Jesus wanted to tell him about freedom, His answer was, **"FREEDOM IN YOUR DECISIONS."** Jesus said Mike didn't have freedom in his decisions at that point. When Mike asked if something was blocking his having freedom in his decisions, Jesus said there was. Then Mike asked, "Can You give me the name of the block?" Before Jesus could answer, Mike said, "Jesus, did You just cause me to laugh?" When Jesus said **"YES,"** Mike asked *why* Jesus had caused him to laugh, and Jesus said, **"IT IS JUST SIMPLE."** Mike asked, "Am I thinking it should be complicated?" When Jesus said **"YES,"** Mike asked if Jesus would tell him why he thought that way.

"YOU NEED TO FIGURE IT OUT."
"In which direction should we head to figure it out?"
"BACKWARD. IT STARTED IN CHILDHOOD."

He asked Jesus to show him what happened when he was a child. Mike saw himself in Latin class, sitting on the left side of the room. A friend was sitting in front of him. The teacher was going down the row, asking questions. Mike felt a little anxiety. When she got to his friend, she got on to him because he answered the question wrong and used bad grammar. Mike took up for his friend. She gave his friend a lick because he used bad grammar. Then, she gave Mike a choice- a switch or a paddle because he had taken up for his friend. Mike took a lick and laughed about it. Mike asked, "Lord, when she gave me a choice, how did I perceive that?" Jesus said it was his decision, his choice. He had to pick one or the other. Mike asked if he had a feeling that when he had to make choices, the choices were all bad ones. Jesus said he felt that way a lot of the time. He also said that when Mike had to make a decision, he felt he sometimes had to pick the one *least* bad. Jesus indicated there was something else He wanted Mike to get out of this-freedom of choices. He said that choices are not necessarily bad if they are wrong; they are not necessarily followed by punishment even if they are wrong.

"Then the feeling I have is if I make a wrong decision, I will be punished?"
"THAT IS CORRECT."
"How can I be healed of this feeling?"
"UNDERSTAND IT."

Jesus said He had not yet given Mike all he needed to understand it.

"Then, Lord, what is the next thing You need to reveal to me?"
"INFLUENCES- CHILDHOOD AND TEENAGE INFLUENCES, PEOPLE."

Jesus indicated he wanted to take these one by one. Mike asked who he should look at first. Jesus said Mike's mother- that she wasn't always right, but Mike had thought she was. His thinking she was always right made him feel he always had to be right.

"SHE DIDN'T UNDERSTAND YOUR DECISION ABOUT THE MINISTRY, BUT YOU DIDN'T KNOW THAT."
"Lord, how did her not understanding affect me?"
"SHE SAW IT AS GLORIOUS, AS A PASTOR, AS A HERO. YOU PICKED UP ON THAT AND YOU DIDN'T WANT TO DISAPPOINT HER."
"Do I equate making the wrong decision with disappointing her?"
"JUST IN THE MINISTRY."
"How has this programming affected my ministry?"
"UNATTAINABLE GOALS."
"Lord, is it like, no matter what I do, I can't win?"
"YES. THE PLANE WILL CRASH EVENTUALLY."

"Lord, if You equate this to a plane crash, where am I right now?"
"SPUTTERING."

When Mike asked who Jesus wanted him to look at next, Jesus gave him the name of a man who had meant a lot to him. When he asked how this man fit in, Jesus said, **"YOU ADMIRED HIM AND YOU DON'T WANT TO DISAPPOINT HIM."**
Mike asked what would cause him to disappoint his friend.

"THAT IS SIMPLE. LEAVE THE PULPIT."
"What does that have to do with my freedom?"
"YOU FEEL LIKE YOU DO BECAUSE YOU DON'T HAVE THE FREEDOM NOT TO. YOU DON'T HAVE A CHOICE."
"Are You saying I really *do* have a choice?"
"YES."
"Lord, do You want to tell me anything else about my friend?"
"HE DIDN'T FULLY UNDERSTAND THE CALL."
"Lord what really was my call?"
"FEED MY SHEEP."
"What does that mean, Lord?"
"SERVING. YOU HAVE THE FREEDOM NOT TO."

When Mike asked if he really did have that freedom, Jesus said, **"YES."** Mike asked, if he could understand that at a heart level, what difference it would make in his life. Jesus said he would serve because he chose to. When Mike asked Jesus to describe how he had been serving, Jesus said, **"SENSE OF MY CALLING, BUT MISUNDERSTANDING."** Mike asked Jesus to tell him what he had misunderstood. Jesus said, **"THE CHOICE IS YOURS; YOU COULD SERVE OR NOT SERVE."**

"Lord, why does it seem we are going around in a circle?"
"THATISWHATYOUNEEDTOUNDERSTAND. IT IS A PATTERN. DIFFERENT PEOPLE, SAME PATTERN."

Mike said it had to do with a lot of people. If he didn't get an award, he hadn't done what he was supposed to do. In the Church of God, he and a friend were brought before the church because they had gone to a movie on Sunday afternoon. They asked if he went to the movie and he lied. His friend told the truth and was kicked out of the church. Another time, He was sitting on the front pew and was chastised for writing in his Bible.

Mike family was poor, but his friends were in the upper echelon. They had cars and he didn't. He was on the ball team and most of them were, so he got to hang out with them.

"Lord, what was the message I got out of that?"
"THAT YOU WEREN'T LIKE THEM AND YOU WEREN'T PERFECT. YOU HAD THE FEELING YOU HAD TO BE PERFECT."

Mike asked if in Jesus' eyes he had to be perfect. Jesus said, **"YOU DON'T HAVE TO BE PERFECT. I AM PERFECT."** Mike said, "Lord, if I'm not perfect, what do I feel will happen?" Jesus said Mike felt people wouldn't understand. Mike asked, "and what do I feel will happen if they don't understand?" Jesus said Mike felt there would be

bad consequences, bad results, and they wouldn't like him and he would lose the progress he
had made.

"Lord, is this true?"

"NOT THE WAY I DEFINE IT. I DEFINE IT AS RELAXATION, ENJOYMENT, SATIS-FACTION, FULFILLMENT."

He said Mike felt people had to respect him in order to have those things. He went on to say that Mike concentrated too much on trying to get people to respect him and that was wrong. When Mike asked why that was wrong, Jesus said, **"YOU ARE THE MESSENGER, JUST THE MESSENGER. THEY HAVE TO TRUST ME, NOT YOU.** Mike said, "Are You saying I have to trust You and not them?" Jesus said, **"YES."**

When Mike asked Jesus to describe the main problem he was facing, Jesus said, **"FREEDOM TO ENJOY YOUR WORK WITHOUT FEELING FORCED, WITHOUT FEELING CHAINED, WITHOUT FEELING YOU WILL BE PUNISHED IF YOU DON'T."**

This was our last session. Today, Mike reports he continues to pastor a church, and in addition, through his counseling and teaching ministry, "feeds Jesus' sheep," and he does all of this ministry with a freedom he had not experienced before. The work he does today has been his own choice, and he says he's the happiest he has ever been. He *is* excellent at what he does, and obviously enjoys everything he is doing.

Satan would have liked for Mike to not realize how much anger he was carrying toward God. By doing that, he could have caused him to continue to see his ministry as a heavy burden, which would have kept him from the power he received by being set free.

Satan is a persistent foe, but the truth is, Satan has no power but the power we give him. He has already been defeated by Jesus. One of the primary ways we give Satan power is through an unforgiving spirit. We also give him power when we meditate on negative things. We give him power when we take our eyes off God.

13.

Ancestral Bonds

There are many things about the spiritual realm that we can't know in our earthly existence, but *occasionally* we have received glimpses of that realm as we have helped others seek healing and as we have tried to walk closer with God in our own journey.

A little over 20 years ago, a lady I had worked with from south Georgia. sent me a book, *Healing The Family Tree* by Dr. Kenneth McAll. In the book, Dr. McAll discussed "ancestral bonds," negative traits that come down through families which keep members of a family in bondage. He had proven through his research that by celebrating the Eucharist with a family member, these bonds could be revealed and broken, not only in the individual involved, but also in all family members who had inherited the bond.

I read the book with some interest, but honestly, what Dr. McAll shared was a little frightening to me. It didn't fit with anything I had experienced in my counseling, so I just put the book aside as something interesting, but with no application for our ministry.

It wasn't long after reading the book that we had a client (Barbara) come to whom God revealed that some of the problems she was experiencing were the result of an ancestral bond that had come down through her family. After the session where God revealed this bond to her, I got the book down and reread it. My immediate reaction was to try to help her find healing the same way that Dr. McAll did it- by celebrating the Lord's supper with her, but God indicated strongly that wasn't the way He wanted me to do it. He told me to use the technique He had already shown me of having people ask questions of Him and let Him bring the answers.

When Barbara came, she was carrying the four demons of fear, guilt, insecurity and anger. It was only after we dealt with these that Jesus told her about the ancestral bond. Here is her conversation with Jesus:

"Jesus, do You love me?"
"YES. VERY MUCH."
"Lord, did You send me here?"
"YES, TO DISCOVER WHO YOU ARE AND WHO I AM IN YOU."
"Who am I?"
"A SWEET, CARING LITTLE GIRL."
"Lord, what is this I'm feeling?"
"TREMBLY."
"How long have I carried this feeling with me?"
"A LONG TIME."
"Does this fear go back to when I was in the womb?"
"YES. YOUR MOTHER WAS AFRAID."
"Lord, would it be helpful to know why she was afraid?"
"SHE HAD TWO MISCARRIAGES AND ONE DEAD AT BIRTH."
"Lord, did I pick up on her feelings through the cord?"
"YES. YOU SENSED THE TENSION AND THE STRESS."

"I can see the little baby pulling into a tight ball. Lord, what does that mean?"

"YOU DON'T KNOW WHAT IS HAPPENING."

"Did it make me feel insecure?"

"YES. INSECURE AND FEARFUL.

"Fearful of what?"

"I'M GOING TO INTERPRET IT THROUGH YOUR MOTHER'S MIND. DEATH."

"Fear of death, Lord?"

"YES."

"How has this affected my life, Lord?"

"THINGS HAPPEN- FEELING OF BEING TRAPPED IN A CORNER BY PEOPLE. YOU AND ALL YOUR SIBLINGS HAVE IT."

"Was I insecure?"

"YES. YOU ALWAYS WANTED TO PLEASE."

"In truth, was I insecure in the womb?"

"YES. BECAUSE OF YOUR MOTHER'S FEELINGS."

"Was I in physical danger?"

"NO."

"But, I felt I was?"

"YES. TURMOIL."

"I bought a lie?"

"YES."

"Is death another lie I bought?"

"YES. AND THAT HAS AFFECTED YOUR LATER LIFE."

"How has this affected me?"

"FEAR FOR YOUR CHILDREN. FEAR OF THE DEATH OF RELATIONSHIPS."

"All this fear is based on bad programming in the womb?"

"YES."

"Lord, how can I be healed?"

"START TRUSTING ME."

"Don't I trust You?"

"NOT TOTALLY."

"Can You explain that to me, Lord?"

"FEAR TO LET GO. MIGHT NOT WORK OUT. IF LET GO, MAY HAVE TO GIVE UP."

"If I let go, will things work out?"

"MAYBE NOT TO YOUR SPECIFICATIONS."

"Will they work out in a way that is pleasing to You?"

"EVENTUALLY."

"If I let go, will I have to give up something?"

"YES. YOU WILL HAVE TO GIVE UP PRIDE. CONTROL. YOU.

"What do You mean by "You?"

"ALL I'VE EQUIPPED YOU WITH, YOU WILL HAVE TO GIVE UP. YOU HAVE GOT TO BE WILLING TO BE NOTHING."

"Nothing, so You can be everything?"

(How does that make you feel?)

"Scared because of past failures. Lord, is this fear coming from Satan?"

"YES."

"Lord, what do I do when this fear comes up?"

"DO WHAT I HAVE TOLD YOU TO DO. REBUKE IT AND CALL OUT MY NAME AND STOP MASSAGING THE FEAR."

"Will it be easier now that I know where it is coming from?"

"YES."

"What can I do about the need to be in control?"

"NOTHING. THAT IS WHY YOU ARE SO OUT OF CONTROL."

"I have to totally depend on You?"

"YES."

"This is scary, Lord. I don't want to drop my defense."

"YOU'RE DEFENSELESS ANYWAY."

"What difference will it make if I can drop my defense?"

"EXTREME JOY-INFECTIOUS-CONTAGIOUS. STOP WORRYING SO MUCH ABOUT THINGS YOU CAN'T CONTROL. MOST OF YOUR GUILT IS FALSE."

"If I drop my defense, will the power of the Holy Spirit come into my life?"

"ABSOLUTELY!"

"Lord, would You give me the courage to do what You are asking?"

"ARE YOUR READY? IT WILL BE EXPENSIVE."

"What do You mean, Lord?"

"YOU MAY LOOK FOOLISH."

"Why will I look foolish?"

"YOU WILL BE A TOTALLY DIFFERENT PERSON."

"Satan, I bind you and cast you out in the name of Jesus Christ."

"Lord, did You say I would be a totally different person and may look foolish?"

"NO."

"How can I tell when Satan comes in on the conversation?"

"HE IS ALWAYS TAUNTING AND MEAN-MEAN THOUGHTS."

"I won't look foolish- just different?"

"YES. YOU WILL BE BEAUTIFUL."

"Lord, does my lack of trust go back to the womb?"

"NOT ENTIRELY."

"What do You mean?"

"INSECURITY BEGAN. PEOPLE PLEASING CAME FROM GROWING UP AND WANTING TO PLEASE YOUR PARENTS. YOUR DADDY WAS A PERFECTIONIST. YOU DIDN'T KNOW ME THEN AND YOU WERE SO INSECURE."

"Lord, is there something else You want to show me now?"

"DEAL WITH SATAN- PUTTING IMAGINATIONS IN YOUR MIND."

"What do I need to do to deal with that, Lord?"

"WHEN THOUGHTS AND VAIN IMAGINATIONS COME IN THE FUTURE, CONSCIOUSLY REBUKE THEM AND CALL ON ME."

At the end of this first session, she felt God's peace.

When we started the second session, God told her He wanted her to look at anxiety, that she had been carrying it for years, going back to her early childhood. There had been a lot of activity in their home. Her mother and daddy were always busy. She asked what message she was getting out of this.

"A MESSAGE FOR A LIFETIME. IT NEVER STOPS."

He said that her biting her nails was caused by the anxiety she was feeling.

"Lord, is life just that- a series of busy work?"
"IT HAS BEEN FOR YOU. THE STRUGGLE IN RECENT YEARS IS THAT YOU KNOW OF THE SABBATH REST, BUT LIKE A TREADMILL, LIFE IS LIKE ON A ROLL. YOU

DON'T KNOW WHERE TO GET OFF, AND WHAT YOU DESIRE IS RESTING IN ME."

"Lord, *is* life just a treadmill?"

"NO, NO, NO, AND YOU KNOW NO."

"Lord, if I know "no," why is it still a treadmill?"

"SOMETHING IN YOU IS DRIVING YOU."

"Lord, tell me what is driving me."

"YOU, SATAN, AND A LOT OF OTHER PEOPLE. IT'S PEOPLE'S EXPECTATIONS, AND SATAN'S GAME AND THE FACT THAT IT'S THE ONLY WAY YOU KNOW TO LIVE. YOUR PERFECT PATTERN HAS BEEN YOUR MOM AND *I* SHOULD BE YOUR PATTERN. TO DENY YOUR MOM'S PATTERN IS NOT TO DENY HER. FOR YOU TO LIVE AS I WOULD HAVE YOU LIVE WOULD PLEASE HER MORE THAT ANYTHING. THE JESUS IN YOU COULD POSSIBLY DISPEL OTHERS' EXPECTATIONS. THEY WOULD SEE MORE OF JESUS THAN ANYTHING YOU COULD DO HUMANLY. I KNOW YOU DESIRE TO STUDY MY WORD AND PRAY. YOU GET CAUGHT UP IN OTHER THINGS AND GET FRUSTRATED."

"Lord, is this where some of my anger comes from?"

"YES. YOU HAVE A STRONG DISTASTE FOR LAZINESS. YOU HAVE A JEALOUSY TOWARD PEOPLE WHO ARE NOT INVOLVED AND DON'T FEEL GUILTY ABOUT IT. YOU DON'T FEEL WORTHY UNLESS YOU ARE PRODUCTIVE."

"Lord, tell me how I define the word, "productive.""

"MAKE A LIST, CHECK IT OFF. SEE THE RESULTS, AND NOBODY UPSET."

"Lord, is that the way You want me to be productive?"

"NO. I WANT YOU TO GET FIRST THINGS FIRST AND GET SETTLED IN YOUR SPIRIT."

"How do I do that, Lord?"

"COMING TO GRIPS WITH THESE THINGS DAILY. INTENTIONALLY SEEKING ME DAILY."

"I see a picture of a mother shopping with a baby on a restraint. I have to let Him do that with me. I can't do it without Him. He has to protect me from myself and from others who would use me."

Her third session dealt with a family situation and how to handle it.

We started the fourth session with a question.

"Lord, is it You who has been waking me early in the morning?"

"YES. BUT YOU HAVEN'T REMOVED YOUR-SELF FROM THE ANXIETY YOU FEEL."

"You are awakening me, but the anxiety is coming from someplace else?"

"YES. BECAUSE I WANT YOU TO GET UP AND BE WITH ME AND YOU REFUSE TO DO THAT."

"What am I feeling right now, Lord?"

"FRUSTRATION. GUILT."

"Where are these feelings coming from?"

"THEY ARE NOT COMING FROM ME."

"Are they from me, Lord?"

"YES."

"Why do I put this stuff on myself?"

"THAT PATTERN OF NEGATIVE THINKING YOU HAVE HAD FOR MOST OF YOUR ADULT LIFE."
"Lord, would You take me back to when I got on this track?"

Barbara started seeing pictures of herself coming home from college on weekends, procrastinating about things she needed to do at school. She always dreaded going back on Sunday nights. She hated the responsibility. It seemed she had always hated Mondays.

"Lord, when did hating Mondays start?"
"COLLEGE. BECOMING A RESPONSIBLE ADULT."
"Was that where it came from- just becoming a responsible adult?"
"YOU WEREN'T TAUGHT RESPONSIBILITY GROWING UP. YOU DIDN'T UNDERSTAND SELF-DISCIPLINE."
"Lord, what do I need to do to be healed of this negative thinking pattern?"
"REPENT OF YOUR NEGATIVE THINKING AND BEGIN TO PRAISE. IT WILL HAVE TO BE AN ACT OF YOUR WILL."
"Lord, I repent of my negative thinking. Will You help me to do this?"
"YES, I WILL."
"When I awaken in the morning, will You bring praise to me instead of negative thinking?"
"YES. I WANT YOU TO GET ON UP."
"Why is it important that I get up and visit with You then?"
"I'VE PROVEN TO YOU THAT IS THE BEST TIME OF DAY FOR YOU AND ME."

"Why am I feeling stupid, Lord?"
"BECAUSE YOU KNOW YOU HAVE BEEN DISOBEDIENT."
"Do You want me feeling stupid?"
"NO."

Barbara said she sensed all this was just going back over the same old ground.

"Lord, do You have to go over the same old ground with others?"
"WITH MOST EVERYBODY."
"Is it just part of our humanity?"
"YES, BUT I HAVE CONQUERED YOUR HUMANITY."
"Lord, is there anything else You want to share with me?"
"BE SURE YOU SPEND TIME WITH ME ALONE. YOU NEED EXERCISE, FRESH AIR. YOU NEED TO BE DILIGENT ABOUT YOUR DIETS AT HOME."
"Is there anything else, Lord?"
"LET UP ON EVERYBODY."
"Will You help me do that, Lord?"
"YOU WILL REALLY SEE A DIFFERENCE."

In response to her question about who "everybody" included, Jesus listed several specific people Barbara needed to let up on. These were people she was angry with. He told her that being angry with them wouldn't fix the situation, and there was no way she could fix *them*. He told her she should **"HANG IN THERE AND PERSEVERE IN LOVE."**
When she asked what she could do with the anger she was feeling, He told her to give it to Him. She visualized herself pouring all her anger into a garbage bag and giving

it to Him. He tied a knot in the top of the bag and threw it away. Then He embraced Barbara. Jesus told her this would do it for now, but she should come back when she sensed frustration and distress.

When she came back four months later, Jesus told her that it was His will that she return in order to deal with her anger.

It turned out her anger was caused by an ancestral bond that went back to her grandfather on her father's side. The bond of anger came from pride and self-protection. God told her the bond had also come down through some of the grandchildren, but not all of them. It went back to the 1929 depression. Her grandfather was a high achiever with a strong desire to not fail.

When she asked Him to break the bond, Jesus said He had broken the bond in her and in her siblings. He said the reason it continued to be a problem for her was because it was her point of weakness in the flesh. Barbara said, "What needs to be done?

She was to go back to the place where she grew up and to pray over the house where they had lived. She was to bind the enemy and she was to tell her siblings about what she was planning to do.

He told her the pride had also come down through her mother's side. It showed itself in not wanting people to fix her, but wanting to fix others.

He told her He was breaking that bond in her and also in her siblings.

She asked why she had such a hard time receiving love.

"YOU'VE ALWAYS WANTED TO GIVE IT OUT MORE THAN TO RECEIVE IT. WHEN YOU GIVE, IT MAKES YOU FEEL GOOD

AND YOU CAN ASSERT YOURSELF. BUT TO RECEIVE, TAKES HUMILITY."

"Lord, would You define humility for me?"

"TOTALLY SUBMISSIVE TO THE FATHER."

"Lord, are You saying it has nothing to do with my actions or with other people?"

"HUMILITY IS BETWEEN YOU AND ME. HUMILITY HAS TO DO WITH YOUR BEING UNDER MY AUTHORITY, NOT HOW YOU RESPOND TO SOMEBODY."

"Lord, if I learn to let Your will be my will, will all the other stuff fall into place?"

"YES."

"Lord, do I have a hard time accepting help from You?"

"YES. YOU THINK YOU ARE SO STRONG. YOU GET THAT FROM YOUR MOTHER. YOU GO DO WHAT I'VE DIRECTED YOU TO DO TODAY AND YOU WILL BE SET FREE."

Barbara was obedient in doing what God had directed, and she was set free.

Jesus has indicated to a number of people that, when ancestral bonds are broken, they are not only broken in members of the family who are still living, but also in those who have passed on. I realize this is a strange concept for many. In order to try to understand it, we have to accept the fact that death is not an ending, but a transition, with our physical body dying and our soul living on. I believe when we get to the other side, when we see God face to face; we will see *truth* face to face. All preconceived notions and ideas and programming will be gone. Paul gives us some light on this, in his letter to the Corinthians (1 Corinthians 13:12) when he wrote, "For now, we see through a glass, darkly; but then face to face: now I know in part; but then shall I know even as also I am known."

From what Jesus has shown us as we have dealt with ancestral bonds, when people die in the bond, they don't realize how bound they are while they are still in their earthly bodies. On the other side, they are able to see not only the bond, but how it affected their earthly existence and how it has affected the other members of their family, including those still living. I believe, at that point, wherever their souls are, they are in prayer that some member of their living family will break that bond by acknowledging it and asking God to break it. For some reason, it seems important that the binding and loosening be done *on earth.*

Matthew 16:19 tells us "...and whatsoever thou shalt bind on earth shall be bound in heaven: and whatsoever thou shalt loose on earth shall be loosed in heaven."

Many times, in working with clients dealing with ancestral bonds, we will have them ask Jesus if their loved ones who have gone on have been praying that the ancestral bond would be broken in their family. The answer is *always* **"YES."** After the bond is broken, we usually have them ask, "Is there rejoicing in heaven today because this bond has been broken in our family?" Again, the answer *always* received is **"YES."**

Since working with Barbara, we have had everyone we've worked with over any length of time ask God if there are any ancestral bonds which have come down through their family which need to be dealt with. It seems that most families have been bound to some extent. If Jesus indicates there *is* a bond, clients ask on which side of the family it has come down- father's or mother's. When that's determined, they ask how many generations back the bondage goes. Once that's known, they ask God to show them what went on at that time that caused the bond to start.

Recently I worked with a divorced lady I've worked with many times over several years. After we asked Jesus about some things going on in her life, she asked if there was anything else. She felt there was something else, but she wasn't getting any answer. She asked if there was a barrier between them and Jesus indicated she was afraid to look at the truth.

"Please show me what I am afraid to look at."
"THE POSSIBILITY OF BEING ALONE THE REST OF YOUR LIFE."
"How has this affected my life?"
"YOU THINK YOU ARE MISSING SOME-THING AND THAT PEOPLE LOOK DOWN ON YOU BECAUSE OF THAT."
"So, I'm concerned about what people might think?"
"YES."

When she asked if He would touch and heal her right then, He said He would.

She then asked if people really do look down on her because she is not married. Jesus said that was a lie from Satan trying to pull her down. He assured her she was missing *no good thing*. When she asked if she has lived with the thought that she was missing something in her life, He said she had. He told her it had to do with an ancestral bond that had come down on her father's side that went back eight generations.

When she asked Jesus to show her what had happened eight generations back, she had a vision of the time of the War between the States. The father had gone off to war. The children had to run everything alone and they never had enough food, clothes, or anything else. There was a lot of uncertainty about having what they needed. When she asked

152

Jesus how this had affected her family since then, He said it was the feeling that no matter what they had, it would never be enough.

Jesus said He wanted to break the bond and He was doing it right then. He said it was broken in each living member of her family and it was also broken in those who had died in the bond. Those who had died did not realize they were bound until they reached the other side. At that point, they could see all truth, and could see the bond. They had been praying that someone in the family would break the bond. He told her there was rejoicing in heaven over the bond finally being broken.

When she asked what difference this would make in her life, Jesus said,

"I WILL PROVIDE WHAT YOU NEED TO MAKE YOU HAPPY AND WHAT YOU DON'T NEED WOULDN'T MAKE YOU HAPPY ANYWAY."

One of the most interesting cases involving the breaking of an ancestral bond had to do with Paul Johnson. We worked with Paul a number of sessions prior to the one where the ancestral bond was revealed. We've lost track of Paul, so we've changed enough of his story that we believe only he will be able to tell it's his.

In talking with Paul about an ancestral bond, Jesus indicated that there are times when we should pray for the dead, and that it is possible for prayer after the death of a loved one to accomplish salvation. I realize there is no scriptural reference to this, but it is a very loving concept. Paul's healing also involved repenting for an ancestor. We don't ask that you believe these concepts; we do pray you will have an open mind about them.

Paul was a Christian who, in the past, had problems with alcohol. When he came for counseling, he had conquered that addiction but had become addicted to prescription drugs- any drug he could get his hands on that was mind-numbing. He shared with us that when he visited friends and went into their bathrooms, he would check their medicine cabinet to see if he could find any painkilling pills. When he found some, he would steal a few. He said he couldn't understand why he kept doing this, but that he seemed *compelled* to do it.

In a session in 1991, God indicated He needed to talk with Paul about an addictive behavior which had come down to him through his family. He revealed this had come down through seven generations. and that He would show Paul what had happened seven generations back that had set up this bond in his family. Paul then heard the word, "ship," and asked God if this had to do with something that happened on a ship. Getting an affirmative answer, he asked if God would give him another word that would give him some indication as to what God was talking about. He got the word, **"BONDAGE."** He then asked if it had anything to do with a slave ship. The answer was **"NO."**

Paul asked, "What kind of bondage are You talking about?" God revealed there had been a relative who was an indentured servant serving aboard a ship. It was a miserable, lowly, horrible existence. On those ships, spirits in kegs, like rum or gin, were always available to the crew. It was easy to obtain. Paul said he was able to sense the man was able to ease his pain from being in bondage and away from his family by partaking of these spirits. He was actually substituting one bondage for another.

Paul asked if there was anything else about this he needed to know. God indicated the man died in the bondage and never became free of it. This relative did not die at sea and did not have a Christian burial. He had became ill at sea, came into port, and died in a rented room, totally alone. He was buried in an unmarked pauper's grave.

Paul asked if it would be helpful for him to know this relative's name. God said, "**WILLIAM.**"

"Lord, can You explain how this has bound our family for seven generations?
"**IT IS BECAUSE HE WAS IN BONDAGE TO MAN AND THEN TO DRINK, BUT NEVER SOUGHT MY HELP, AND HE DIED IN THAT BONDAGE.**"
"How did I get related to him?"
"**BEFORE HE WAS INDENTURED, HE HAD A WIFE AND A CHILD AND HE LOST EVERYTHING DUE TO POOR BUSINESS PRACTICES, THEN WAS INDENTURED AND TAKEN AWAY FROM HIS FAMILY. THE MARRIAGE WAS NOT A GOOD ONE BECAUSE HE HAD BEEN A POOR PROVIDER AND HIS WIFE WAS GLAD TO BE RID OF HIM. THE CHILD OF THAT MARRIAGE WAS ONE OF YOUR GREAT GRANDFATHERS. THE LACK OF HAVING A FATHER IN THE HOME AS WELL AS THE EARLY PAINFUL REMEMBRANCES AND ALSO THE RIDICULE THAT THIS CHILD SUFFERED BECAUSE OF THE SITUATION HE WAS PLACED IN DUE TO HIS FATHER'S FAILINGS CAUSED GREAT REJECTION AND PAIN WHICH HE ALSO TRIED TO DROWN WITH SPIRITS.**"

God revealed the bond had come down through Paul's father's side. Paul asked if the bond had affected every generation.

"**YES. SOME MORE THAN OTHERS. THERE HAS BEEN A TENDENCY IN EVERY MALE**

CHILD IN YOUR LINE GOING BACK TO THE PERSON WILLIAM JOHNSON, TO ESCAPE ANY UNCOMFORTABLE, UNPLEASANT, OR PAINFUL EXPERIENCE OR FEELING WITH SOME REMEDY OTHER THAN ME. SOME USE FOOD. MANY HAVE USED SEX, AND MANY, MANY HAVE USED DRUGS OR ALCOHOL."

"Lord, what do You want me to do to break this bondage that William brought on our family?

"YOU HAVE TO REPENT FOR WILLIAM, FOR HE NEVER REPENTED."

"Lord, how do you repent for someone else?

God showed him a grave. Paul asked what that meant.

"THE GRAVE REPRESENTS THE DEATH THAT HAS COME TO ALL IN YOUR LINEAGE GOING BACK TO WILLIAM BECAUSE OF THE BONDAGE. IT WAS A TYPE OF DEATH INTO WHICH MY FULL LIFE COULD NOT ENTER BECAUSE OF THE BONDAGE BROUGHT DOWN FROM GENERATION TO GENERATION. AND, SATAN HAS USED THE DARK AREA IN EACH MALE'S LIFE BACK TO WILLIAM TO KEEP EACH OF THEM FROM REACHING THE FULL POTENTIAL I HAVE HAD FOR ALL THE FAMILY. THERE HAVE EVEN BEEN THOSE WHO HAVE ANSWERED THE CALL THAT I HAVE PLACED ON EACH SUCCEEDING GENERATION TO DO MY WORK, BUT THEY TOO HAVE BEEN LIMITED BY THE DARKNESS THAT HAS EXTENDED OVER TIME."

Paul asked God if it would be helpful for him to know which country William grew up in.

"ENGLAND."

Now, Paul asked specifically how he could repent for William. He was told to take his father and his son and go to his grandfather's grave which was in a nearby town, and together they were to repent for William. Next, he was to go to his great-grandfather's grave in a neighboring state. God said it was okay if his father and son also went to this grave, but it wasn't necessary. Paul asked again, "When we get to the grave, how do we repent for William?" God assured him that He would give him the words to say.

Paul asked if God would prepare his father's heart and his son's heart to accept this. God indicated that his Father's heart was already prepared, and that He was in the process of preparing his son's heart.

Paul next asked if all this would have any effect on the soul of William.

"IT'S INTERESTING THAT YOU ASK THAT. DO YOU REMEMBER THE RECENT CONVERSATION YOU HAD WITH YOUR WIFE IN WHICH YOU TOLD HER THAT YOU FELT THERE WAS A PLACE IN WHICH LOST SOULS COULD BE PLACED, WHERE PRAYER AFTER DEATH COULD ACCOMPLISH SALVATION?"

"Lord, is this really true?"

"YES AND THOUGH THERE IS NO DIRECT SCRIPTURAL REFERENCE TO THIS, BECAUSE IT IS A CONFUSING CONCEPT TO THE MIND OF MEN AS IT RELATES TO WHAT I HAVE TAUGHT REGARDING

SALVATION WHILE ALIVE. AT THIS TIME, I WON'T ELABORATE FURTHER EXCEPT TO TELL YOU BOTH TO CONTINUE IN PRAYING FOR THOSE WHO HAVE GONE ON WHEN MY SPIRIT MOVES YOU TO SO PRAY."

Paul asked if there was anything else he needed to do after he had visited the two graves and repented for William. God told him he needed to go and visit each surviving family member and share God's love. Paul asked if, when he did this, it would heal his entire family. God told him it would, and he would see miraculous changes in *many* of his family members. God told him he wouldn't fully realize the miraculous changes in some because he hadn't been close enough to them to know the problems they suffer.

"ONE THING YOU NEED TO UNDERSTAND IS THAT THE HEALING WILL ONLY TAKE AWAY THE *DESIRE* TO SEEK ESCAPE. IT IS NOT A LICENSE TO SEEK THE WAYS OF THE WORLD. IN OTHER WORDS, YOUR FAMILY, AND THIS GOES FOR ALL MY CHILDREN, NEED TO STEER CLEAR OF MIND ALTERING SUBSTANCES."

Paul then asked God if this bond that had started with William had anything to do with the fact that there was a lack of success in the Johnson family.

"YES, THE BONDAGE THAT KEPT WILLIAM FROM REACHING ANY POTENTIAL HAS BEEN VISITED ON EACH SUCCEEDING GENERATION. IT STARTED WHEN HE FAILED BEFORE HE WAS EVER PLACED IN INDENTURED SERVICE. SATAN USED THE FAILURE TO DESTROY HIM AND TO

DESTROY MY WILL FOR SUCCESS, AND
WHEN I SAY SUCCESS, I DON'T ONLY
MEAN MATERIAL SUCCESS, BUT I MEAN
SUCCESS IN PUTTING FORTH KINGDOM
PRINCIPLES TO OTHERS. THERE HAS BEEN
A CALL, A STRONG CALL TO MINISTRY,
TO EVANGELISM, TO APOSTOLIC FAITH
BUILDING MINISTRY IN YOUR FAMILY
LINE. THE FAILURE THAT WILLIAM
EXPERIENCED WAS CAUSED BY DIRECT
DEMONIC ATTACK INTO HIS LIFE TO
DESTROY THAT WHICH SATAN SAW
WILLIAM WAS BEGINNING TO DO. THE
TIME NOW IS GROWING LATE AND I AM
SETTING MY PEOPLE FREE. IT HAS NEVER
BEEN MORE URGENT THAT THESE BLOOD
LINE FAMILY BONDAGES BE BROKEN OFF
THOSE WHO I HAVE APPOINTED TO USHER
IN MY RETURN AND THE KINGDOM AGE
SOON TO COME ON THIS EARTH. YOUR
SUCCESS IS NECESSARY FOR THE FREEING
OF MANY OTHERS. YES, YOUR FAMILY
HAS SUFFERED MUCH AND HAS SUFFERED
LACK BECAUSE OF THE BONDAGE THAT I
HAVE YEARNED TO DELIVER THEM FROM
BUT YOU ARE THE FIRST TO WALK IN AN
UPRIGHT WAY AND TO SEEK HARD ENOUGH
FOR ME TO BE ABLE TO SHOW YOU THE
CAUSE. YOU ARE TYPICAL OF MANY, MANY
OF MY SERVANTS. THERE ARE MANY WHO
ARE BEING RAISED UP JUST AS YOU AND
BECAUSE OF THE HEAVIER INFLUENCE OF
MY SPIRIT IN THIS DAY, WILL ALSO SEEK
MY REVELATION OF HOW TO BE FREE.

AND I WILL USE YOU AND CHARLES TO FREE MANY."

Although we met for several sessions after this, this session was the most revealing, most dramatic, and I believe, the most healing.

We've lost track of Paul over the past 15 years. The last thing we heard about him was that he was in Seminary, and this was a number of years ago. We believe that he answered the call from God to go into the ministry.

At times, there may be multiple ancestral bonds binding a family. Such was the case of Jason, a Christian pastor who was frustrated and depressed, which are not abnormal feelings for a minister because few ministers seem to have anyone with whom they can vent.

Over a number of sessions, it was revealed there were at least three ancestral bonds which had come down through his family to him. The first went back to the 1600s. A curse had been placed on his father's family by a black woman who was raped by one of his ancestors in Virginia. This ancestral bond had manifested itself in Jason's family in a general feeling of anxiety. Jason asked if healing for this bond had already started. Jesus said it was being effected, but not yet accomplished; that, as Jason exhibited the fruits of the spirit, the power of the curse was being diminished.

Jesus indicated the curse had been placed on his family through devil worship which had been practiced in the black woman's homeland. Jason's ancestor was a hard-hearted man who had never asked Jesus to forgive him for what he had done. When Jason asked if it would be helpful for him to ask for forgiveness for his ancestor, Jesus said it would be.

Jason said, "On behalf of my ancestor, who I don't even know, I ask for forgiveness for him. I pray for this woman and her family and for the effects it may had had on her family. I pray that You might go back in time and stand by that woman when it happened. Break that trauma in her life. And, Lord, I pray that you might stand by my ancestor and convict him of the sin." Jesus said this petition was sufficient.

At another time, Jesus told Jason he had brought him here for counseling to break strongholds and tear down dominions. When he asked which strongholds in his life needed to be torn down, Jesus said, "**DEPRESSION, PASSIVITY, TIMIDITY AND FEAR.**" Jesus went on to tell him this stronghold had been a part of his life from the day he had been conceived. He had been open to the sadness and hurt of generations.

This had occurred because of another ancestral bond that had come down through his grandmother and her family. It was caused by trauma going back to a time when his grandmother's brother accidentally killed a lady.

"YOUR UNCLE ACCIDENTALLY KILLED A LADY ONE SUNDAY AFTERNOON WHILE YOUR GRANDMOTHER WAS AT THEIR HOME. SHE BECAME OBSESSED BY DEATH AND SICKNESS. WITH THE SADNESS AND FRIGHT CAME AN ACCOMPANYING SPIRIT OF GUILT THAT HAS PASSED FROM ONE GENERATION TO THE NEXT AND THIS IS FALSE GUILT."

When Jason asked Jesus if He wanted to heal his family of this curse, Jesus said it had been his purpose *forever*. He said it would take the power of the blood of Jesus and the ministry of the Holy Spirit for it to be broken. When Jason asked if He had already healed his family, Jesus said, **"THE HEALING IS THERE. YOU JUST NEED TO POSSESS IT."** He said Jason could possess the healing by looking unto Him, believing in the healing and receiving it. Jesus told him his depression had been based on a lie. He said, **"YOUR**

FAMILY HAS BEEN DECEIVED BY THE DECEIVER AND YOU HAVE PASSED IT ON ONE GENERATION TO THE NEXT." Jesus said the bond could be broken in other family members *if they desired it.*

Jason went on to ask if the bond had caused his passivity.

"YES, TO AN EXTENT. IT CAUSES YOU TO HESITATE AND OFTENTIMES TO DO NOTHING WHEN THERE IS A CLEAR CALL OF ACTION CALLED FOR."

In another session, Jesus said He wanted to deal with the subject of Jason's anger. He said the bond of anger had started four generations back. Jesus showed Jason a vision of an man beating a mule. A little man came along and grabbed the stick out of the man's hand, knocked the man down, and started kicking him. Jesus said the little man was an ancestor, and this incident was where the bond of anger had started in their family. He said it was a distorted concept of justice filled with violence and lack of self-control. He had jumped on the man because he did not want to see the animal mistreated. Because of the tremendous release of anger, the little man became demonized by other spirits. Jason asked how this had manifested itself in his family.

"BY PRESENTING ANGER AS RIGHTEOUS INDIGNATION AND BY CAUSING YOU TO THINK THAT IN EVERY OCCASION, YOU ARE CORRECT IN THE SITUATION."

Jesus said there could be healing by renouncing anger, violence, rage, and self-righteousness in Jesus name, by commanding that it leave him.

There is one additional thing that came out in our sessions with Jason that I want to share with you. In this session, Jesus was talking about the spiritual world. He said, **"IF YOU COULD SEE THE UNSEEN WORLD, YOU WOULD SEE MY EMISSARIES ALMOST EVERYWHERE, AT ALL TIMES. OFTENTIMES, IN TIMES OF GREAT DISTRESS, AND TIMES OF TRAVAIL OF THE SOUL, I ALLOW THOSE ANGELS TO BE SEEN THAT AN UNBELIEVING GENERATION MIGHT BELIEVE."**

14.

Purpose

One of the really exciting things about having clients talk with God is that God can reveal the purpose for which they were created. There have been times when what He revealed was so real, the client acted on it immediately with great results. The most miraculous instance of this happening occurred when we were working with Karen.

Karen and her husband, a Christian minister, came for therapy a little over 15 years ago. We worked with each of them over a three day period.

Karen's six relatively short sessions here have continued to be one of the high points of our ministry. In the time we were together, God not only brought healing, but revealed specifically why she was created and set her on a course that has led to a very important life work as a Christian Counselor.

Karen was a vivacious young lady. She had been very successful in business. At that time, she was in charge of personnel for a large corporation.

We started the first session by her asking Jesus if He loved her.

"YOU KNOW THAT I DO."
"Do I need healing?
"YES. YOU NEED HEALING OF THE EMOTIONS."
"What emotions do You want to work with first?
"CHILDHOOD. SELF-WORTH. SELF-ESTEEM. ACCEPTANCE."
"Lord, how long have I had a problem with self-worth?"
"ALL YOUR LIFE."
"Did it start while I was in the womb?"
"YES."

Jesus went on to tell her that her mother had only been 18 and not married when she got pregnant with Karen. She was scared, wanted to run and hide, but didn't know what to do. She didn't want a baby. Karen had picked up on her mother's hurts through the umbilical cord and interpreted the feelings as her mother not wanting *her*, which was the origin of her feelings of self-condemnation. He said that this made Karen feel that she wasn't acceptable and that nothing about her was right.

Karen then asked if she had been with Jesus before she was conceived. He said she had been and He knew her characteristics and He loved her.

"Lord, was it Your will that I be born to my mother?"
"YES. YOU ARE A PRECIOUS CHILD. SHE WAS THE ONE I CHOSE. NOT THE METHOD, BUT THE PURPOSE."
"Lord, are You saying I have been chosen, and You allowed me to be born to her for a reason?"
"YES. THROUGH A WEAK BEGINNING, I WILL MAKE YOU STRONG."

"Lord, why did it have to hurt so much?"
"SO YOU COULD SEE THE HURTS IN OTHERS. SO YOU COULD FOCUS ON THEIR NEEDS AND FEEL AND HELP."
"Then, nothing about my life has been a mistake?"
"THAT'S RIGHT. YOU ARE MY PRECIOUS CHILD."

Karen had been adopted at birth. She asked several questions about her birth mother. Jesus told her it wasn't important that she know anything about her, that her mother was now married and had no other children.

Karen suddenly felt a deep sense of loneliness. She asked if that was what she had felt for nine months in the womb. Jesus said it was, and it had caused her to not let people know who she was; she keeps part of herself hidden. He went on to tell her she did this because she feared if people really knew her, they would reject her. He told her this was not true.

She then asked if she had been programmed to *feel* people don't like her. Jesus said she had been. She said, "How do I handle it when people *do* like me?" He said, **"YOU REACT ON THE SURFACE, BUT UNDERNEATH, IT IS NOT REAL."** He told her she has a difficult time accepting the fact that people like her; she didn't feel she was worthy, and, if she revealed her real self to them, they would leave.

At that point, she asked Jesus if He would take on Himself any part of her pain that she couldn't handle. He was now holding her and had His hand on her forehead. She asked why He was doing that.

"TO BLESS YOU. TO TOUCH YOU. TO LET YOU KNOW HOW MUCH I LOVE YOU. TO LOOK AT YOU AS LOVE."
"Are You bringing healing for the terrible sense of loneliness I have carried?"

**"I WILL GIVE YOU STRENGTH. I WILL
BRING PEOPLE TO YOU. YOU WILL BRING
THEM LOVE. YOU WILL HAVE STRENGTH.
I HAVE SPOKEN TO YOU. I HAVE CLAIMED
YOU. I WILL HOLD YOU IN THE PALM OF
MY HAND."**

He ended the session by granting her His peace. He said
He loved her mother and was also giving His peace to her.
He told Karen it was not necessary for her to find out who
her mother was even though she had a strong compulsion to
do so. Her compulsion came because of wanting to know as
much about herself as she could. He told her she could do
that through Him.

She asked if she was going to find healing in our time
together. He told her that she would be totally healed by the
time we were completed.

As we started our second session, Karen and Jesus dealt
for some time with some personal things concerning her
adoptive mother, and a friend. After that, Karen asked if
Jesus had anything else to reveal to her.

**"THAT YOU ARE COMPLETE AS YOU ARE
AND I AM PERFECTING YOU ON THIS
JOURNEY."**
"What journey are You talking about"
**"THE JOURNEY OVER THE NEXT YEARS
YOU HAVE ON THIS EARTH. I WILL USE
YOU MIGHTILY AND MY LOVE WILL BE
MANIFESTED IN YOU."**
"Will I need more training for what You want me to
do?"
**"YES. I WANT YOU TO HAVE TRAINING
SOON. I WANT YOU**

TO BEGIN SOON."

Karen told me she felt God was telling her to go back to college and get a degree in Psychology in order to help His hurting people.

"What do You want me to take, Lord?"
"I WANT YOU TO TAKE AS MANY COURSES AS YOU CAN. I WANT YOU TO QUIT YOUR JOB AND GO BACK TO SCHOOL AND GET YOUR DEGREE."

She asked if they would be able to afford her doing this. He said that He would provide in a mighty way, and she was to follow His plan and act on it.

As her Counselor, this was very frightening to me. It would be a *major* step in her life. I knew that Satan sometimes comes in on God's conversations and can sound just like God, so I had her say, "Satan, I bind you and cast you out in the name of Jesus Christ!" (Over time, I had learned that when I have a question about whether the answer we get is really from God, I could have the client bind Satan and cast him out in Jesus' name and then repeat the question. If we got the same answer both times, it was a good indication the answer was really from God.) She asked Jesus if He had really told her to quit her job. His answer was, **"YES."**

Recently, when I talked with Karen and asked if I could use her story in this book, she reminded me of something I had forgotten. The day after God had revealed she should quit her job and go back to school, He confirmed that message in the session we had with her husband. Jesus also told him it was what He wanted her to do. She said this made it much easier for her to make the decision she did.

Karen's third session started with some questions concerning some of her family members.

Karen then asked Jesus why she had such a hard time sleeping the night before. He told her she had a tendency to jump ahead. He also told her that if she had rested in Him, she could have rested. She asked if this was something He wanted her to learn.

"YES. IF YOU FOCUS ON ME AND WHAT I'M DOING, IT WILL COME TO PASS. DON'T BE ANXIOUS. YOU WANT SO MUCH CONTROL. RELINQUISH IT."

"Lord, are You saying I don't have to make things happen?"

"YES. IT IS NOT UP TO YOU TO MAKE THINGS HAPPEN. IT IS BY MY MIGHT AND POWER."

Changing the subject, she asked, "When should I quit my job?" He told her He wanted her to quit immediately. She asked if He was saying now, or tomorrow, or when? At that point, she felt a tightness in her chest and asked Him what that was. He told her it was fear and lack of trust.

She asked again, "When should I turn in my resignation?" He said He wanted her to do it the next day. She asked Him how long a notice she should give.

"FOUR MONTHS."

"Will my co-workers understand?"

"TO SOME EXTENT. YOUR LEAVING WILL BE A WITNESS FOR ME. BY YOUR LEAVING WITHOUT HAVING ALL THE ENDS TIED UP NEATLY IN A BOW- NOT KNOWING WHERE YOUR FINANCIAL HELP WILL COME FROM- NOT KNOWING WHERE YOUR FOCUS WILL

BE FOLLOWING SCHOOL. BY LEAVING YOUR FUTURE WITH THE COMPANY AND GOING IN ANOTHER DIRECTION- GOING FROM ONE THAT IS SURE TO ONE THAT IS NOT."

"Lord, are You saying that will witness to them?"

"YES. THE PEOPLE AROUND YOU LOOK FOR FINANCIAL SECURITY. THEY ARE TIED TO THE WORLD. IT WILL CAUSE THEM TO QUESTION WHAT IS HAPPENING."

"Lord, where do my tears come from when I cry with people?"

"FROM ME. THEY ARE MY TEARS. YOU FEEL DEEPLY THEIR NEED TO BE HEALED BY ME."

"Lord, do I need any physical healing?"

"JUST TRUST IN ME."

"Lord, are You saying that if I put my trust in You, I don't have to worry about healing?"

"YES, I AM ALL SUFFICIENT. I HAVE A PLAN AND A PURPOSE FOR YOUR LIFE. I WILL BRING IT TO FRUITION."

At that point she said, "Lord, I really need proof that what I have heard is from You. Can You give me that proof?" He told her that He would bring a sense of peace through all the steps. He told her she would recognize the peace and that others would confirm it.

She still had questions. "But Lord, if this is from me, and I start out on it, what will happen?" He told her that if it *was* from her, it would not come to pass, but that she had to trust Him.

"YOU ARE GOING INTO A MINISTRY OF FAITH. YOU HAVE TO ACT ON FAITH."

Although we met two more times, this is the gist of what Karen was told. She followed Jesus' instructions, called her boss and resigned before she and her husband left this area. Later, I learned that a few months after they returned home, her husband was released from the church where he had been ministering. It took him some time to get relocated, but when he did, it was in a town that had a college offering the exact courses Karen was seeking.

A little over a year later, Karen phoned to tell me she had completed her college work and would be interning with a group of Christian Counseling Centers. A year later, she let me know that the people at the Counseling Center where she had interned was so impressed with her work, they hired her as the chief therapist at their center in a major city in her state.

Today, Karen has her own Christian Counseling Center and offers help and love to the people in her area. I know Jesus is pleased with her obedience to His calling, and for the help she has been to so many others. I feel very fortunate to know her and privileged to have been with her as Jesus brought this healing and direction for her life. Remembering our time together always brings joy to my spirit.

A second person to whom God revealed His purpose was Sally. Sally came in August, 1990. She thought God may have given her the gift of prophesy, but wasn't sure. In our work together, God not only told her why she was created, but also revealed that a lot of her fear came from a traumatic birth. At the end of the session, He showed her a place created for her where she could go be with Him any time.

"Lord, do You show me things before they happen?"
"WHEN YOU ARE READY."
"Please make this clearer, Lord." '
"IT IS A GIFT, BUT YOU ARE NOT ALWAYS READY TO RECEIVE IT."

"Lord, what am I supposed to do when You show me these things?"

"PRAY."

"Does this really make a difference, Lord?"

"WHEN YOU PRAY, YOU ARE OPENING TO MY WORD AND DIRECTION. YOU WILL NOT ALWAYS KNOW WHAT IS GOING TO HAPPEN BUT THERE IS SOMETHING YOU NEED TO GET READY FOR."

"Have I prevented You from showing me some things?"

"MANY TIMES."

"Why have I wanted to cut this off?"

"AFRAID OF WHAT OTHERS WILL THINK."

"How long have I carried this burden, Lord?"

"A LIFETIME."

"Did this start when I was in the womb?"

"AT BIRTH."

"Jesus, if this gets too scary or painful, will You take on Yourself what I can't handle?

"YES."

"Lord, can You show me what happened at birth that made me afraid?""It's that crazy floating feeling! He says I have to feel part of it. They are trying to kill me. The doctor. That's where the pressure comes from- my head. I'm too big. Lord, was he really trying to kill me?"

"THE DOCTOR HAD MADE THE DECISION TO SAVE YOUR MOTHER."

"What kept him from killing me?"

"I DID."

"How did You keep him from killing me?"

"THE FLOATING. THAT TOOK THE PRESSURE AWAY."

"Then, the floating was a gift from You?"

"IT TOOK THE PAIN, BUT GAVE YOU FEAR."

"How had the doctor decided to kill me, Lord?"

"HE APPLIED PRESSURE THAT COULD HAVE CRUSHED YOUR HEAD. THE FLOATING HAS BEEN A GIFT. ALL THESE TIMES WHEN YOU WERE IN PAIN, YOU HAVE ALWAYS BEEN ABLE TO FLOAT AROUND FROM IT. DETACH YOURSELF. WHEN I SAY PAIN, I MEAN HURT."

"I understood the gift of floating at the time?"

"YES. SOME PEOPLE ARE NOT ABLE TO DEAL WITH PAIN AND HURT. THIS WAS MY WAY OF HELPING YOU, TO PROTECT YOU, AND BECAUSE YOU WOULD NEED IT."

"Do I still need it, Lord?"

"YES. IT GIVES YOU STRENGTH AND POWER."

"What do You mean by power, Lord?"

"ABILITY TO OPERATE UNDER CONTROL. YOU DON'T USE IT ENOUGH."

"What is keeping me from using it enough?"

"FEAR."

"Fear of what?"

"FEAR OF SOMETHING BEING WRONG WITH YOU. FEAR OF NOT BEING NORMAL."

"How long have I carried this burden?"

"SINCE BIRTH. THE FEELING COMES FROM OTHERS NOT BEING ABLE TO ACCEPT YOU."

"Not being able to accept what about me, Lord?"

"THAT YOU LOOK DIFFERENT. YOU WERE A BIG BABY AND YOU WERE BLACK AND BLUE."

"I picked up on what they were feeling about me?"
"YES."
"And, what was the message I got?"
"FAT AND UGLY. THAT YOU WERE NOT WANTED. YOU WERE DIFFERENT."
"But, that is a lie, isn't it, Lord?"
"PART OF IT. YOU *ARE* DIFFERENT."
"In what way am I different?"
"EVERYONE IS DIFFERENT. I WANTED YOU DIFFERENT."
"Why did You want me different, Lord?"
"A PURPOSE."
"Can You tell me what that purpose is, Lord?"
"YOU HAVE ALREADY BEEN DOING PART OF THE PURPOSE."
"Can You tell me specifically what that purpose is?"
"YOU HAVE INFLUENCED A LOT OF OTHERS."
"Why am I having a hard time believing that, Lord?"
"BECAUSE YOU GET TIRED OF PEOPLE."

(God then gave her the names of some of the ones she had influenced.)

"I don't know what I'm on. I'm going up and down like on a merry-go-round. A real soft movement. Lord, what's happening? There is just a calmness. I think it's the floating, but it is a calm floating."

"I HAVE TAKEN AWAY THE FEAR OF FLOATING. I HAVE ALSO TAKEN YOU AWAY FROM SATAN."
"Lord, have You given me the gift of prophesy?"
"YES."
"What does that word mean to You?"

"PREPARATION. IT ALLOWS YOU TO COME TO ME FOR DIRECTION. I WON'T ALWAYS TELL YOU WHEN SOMETHING IS GOING TO HAPPEN."

"Why won't You?"

"YOU WOULDN'T BELIEVE ME."

"As time goes on, will I come to believe You more and more?"

"YES. DON'T BE AFRAID."

"Lord, what do I do if fear comes?"

"REMEMBER ME AND PRAY."

"Lord, was I with You before I was conceived?"

"YOU HAVE DOUBTS."

"Even though I have doubts, was I with You?"

"YES."

"Why did You put me in the family You did?"

"THEY NEEDED SOMEONE DIFFERENT. YOU NEEDED THE EXPERIENCES."

"Lord, why does that make me mad with You?"

"IT GOES BACK TO BEING SELFISH AND WANTING THINGS."

"Lord, have I been carrying around anger toward You?"

"YES."

"Is it okay to be mad with You?"

"YES. EVERYONE HAS ANGER. IT IS A GIFT."

"What do You mean, it is a gift?"

"IT IS NOT A GIFT TO ALL PEOPLE, BUT IT IS TO YOU. WHEN YOU GET ANGRY, YOU DO SOMETHING ABOUT A SITUATION YOU NEED TO TAKE CARE OF. SOMETIMES YOU DON'T USE THAT ANGER IN AN APPROPRIATE WAY. WHEN YOU GET ANGRY, YOU NEED TO PRAY SO YOU CAN

RESPOND TO THE ANGER IN CONTROL AND NOT IN REACTIVE WAYS THAT COULD HURT SOMEONE."
"I need to use anger as a trigger to pray?"
"YES. IF YOU DON'T, YOU WILL LET THE ANGER CONTROL YOU AND GIVE SATAN A FOOTHOLD."
"Lord, is there other healing I need?"

Jesus kept insisting she read Psalm 37. He told her the reason for reading this Psalm was so she would stop worrying about people who don't have God. He told her to not worry about the beliefs of her boss, that she was influencing her. She asked if He just wanted her to be the person He created her to be, and He said, **"YES, AND WORK AT PRAYING AND READING MY WORD."**

(After this they covered some relationships of hers)

She said she had been seeing Jesus. They were on a cloud. She asked, "Jesus will You heal me by Your touch?" He said, **"MY DEAR CHILD. I HAVE BEEN DOING THIS ALL THE TIME."** Would You do it right now so I can *know* I am healed? (All this time, Jesus had been holding her.)

"Lord, where are we now? Is there a name for this place?"
"HEAVEN."
"But, I don't see anybody there. He didn't want me to see anybody." "Is this a special place where I can come and talk with You anytime?"
"YES."
"Just as we have been doing today?"
"YES."

God has continued to reveal things in the future to Sally. She has used this gift to be an encourager to me and to others.

15.

Our True Beginning and Abortion

God spoke these words to the prophet Jeremiah, "Before I formed thee in the belly I knew thee." I believe what God said to Jeremiah about his beginning is also true for each of us, because of what God has revealed to some of those He has healed through Self/Rise. Of course, it's impossible to prove this (or many of the other Christian concepts) beyond any shadow of doubt. It can only be confirmed by Jesus through the Holy Spirit. When clients are talking with God, there have been times when I've had them ask if they were with God before they were conceived. The answer to that question has always been, **"YES."**

You may be thinking, "Okay, that may be true, but what difference does it make one way or the other that I was with God before I came here?" It makes a lot of difference to me. Since I came from heaven to start with, when I die, I won't be going to a strange place. I'm convinced when I get to heaven, everything about it will be familiar. It will be like going back home after a long, hard trip.

Because of what Jesus has shown us about our being with God before we came here, we have come to the conclusion that *every life* is precious to God. What I'm going to say next will probably turn off a lot of people.

Ours seems to be a society which does not want to face truth, even though Jesus said the truth would set us free. Whether we want to face it or be in denial of it, **abortion is the killing of a child of God**, and I believe we have put this generation in bondage to Satan through the killing of our children using this procedure.

What strange people we are! We look with horror on societies of the past that sacrificed their children to the gods as they understood them. Today, in our "enlightened" society, we sacrifice our unborn en masse to the god of convenience. While I realize there may be circumstances under which an abortion may be the lesser of two evils, there is no way we can justify the excessive number of abortions in our country.

The reason I believe as I do is because of the great number of people with whom I've worked who have re-experienced being in the womb. In several of the case histories in this book, there are examples of this. After over 20 years of working with people, I've come to the conclusion a fetus is a feeling person *from the moment of conception,* and not just a blob of flesh. To me, it is absurd to attempt to determine through some kind of rationalization the specific point at which a fetus becomes a person. Some seem to feel that a fetus isn't human until a certain length of time has passed after conception. Others seem to feel it's not a person until it's born. Regardless of how you *feel*, I don't think you can honestly argue against the point that a fetus is a *potential* person from the moment of conception.

If you do agree that a fetus is a *potential* person, at what point do you think it's justifiable and moral to end its life?

Because of the counseling experience God has allowed me to have, I've come to believe that doctors who perform large numbers of abortions are no better than the Nazis who ran the death camps in Germany. Actually, *any* abortion is an abomination.

In his excellent book, *Healing the Family Tree,* Dr. Kenneth McAll discusses the need to name "lost" children and to have a baptism service for them in order to commit them to Jesus Christ. "Lost" children are those which are aborted, miscarried, stillborn, or die soon after birth. In his book, Dr. McAll gives several examples where physical healing in the one initiating the baptism has occurred when the "lost" child is given a name and committed to Jesus.

Let me share with you a case which indicates what God thinks about aborted babies.

Because of guilt feelings over past events, Jim was suffering from extreme depression. He had decided to commit suicide by taking an overdose of sleeping pills. His wife, sensing his state of mind, hid the sleeping pills. Jim, unable to face his guilt and unable to commit suicide, had a nervous breakdown. Hallucinating and babbling about being chased by "little people," he ran into the woods behind his home wearing only his underwear.

With the assistance of the family doctor, the Sheriff's department, and Emergency Medical Personnel, he was found three hours later and taken to a hospital where he spent several days regaining his hold on reality.

In our first session, Jim shared with me that, when he was in service, he had impregnated five different women and then aided them in having abortions. In our second session, he was aware of clouds moving away and a bright sun coming out. He saw a door that God told him to walk through. God told him this was the door of freedom- freedom from sin. He saw children there. They were holding out their arms to him. They were happy. They were singing. God told him the children loved him.

He asked God if He was leading him to have a baptism for the children. His answer was, **"YES. I WANT YOU**

TO SEND THEM TO ME. TURN THEM OVER TO
THE HOLY SPIRIT TO BRING THEM." Jim said,
"Lord, besides the baptism, is there anything else I should
do to be made free?" God said, "YOU MUST SAY A
SINCERE AND HONEST CONFESSION- WHAT YOU
DID, AND MAKE NO EXCUSES. JUST TELL IT,
INCLUDING THE ILLEGITIMATE CHILD THAT IS
STILL IN JAPAN. DO NOT LEAVE IT OUT. ON THE
ANNIVERSARY OF THE BAPTISM, I WANT YOU
TO CONFESS IT AGAIN AND REMEMBER THE
CHILDREN." Jim said he saw Jesus on the cross. God
went on, "CHRIST DIED FOR YOU AND YOUR SINS.
I LOVE YOU."

Jim asked if there was anything else God wanted to cover
with him. Jim saw a beautiful light, a beautiful light in the
future. He had a vision of himself resting in a chair, old and
gray and happy.

God revealed that, in order to be healed, he needed to
name these aborted children and go to his church and have a
baptism service for each of them.

He spent some time composing a special baptism ceremony, which was beautiful, and each child was symboli-
cally baptized. He gave them Christian names: Samuel,
Ester, Daniel, Ruth and Nathan. He had two friends and his
wife assist in the service. From doing as God had directed
concerning the children, he received healing.

It has now been some time since the special baptism
service for the children, and Jim has enjoyed the healing and
God's promise for the future.

It is obvious that God considers fetuses to be children no
matter at what point they are miscarried, stillborn, die soon
after birth or are aborted.

16.

Healing and God's Revelation

When Anne first came, in April, 1991, she was a 17-year-old young lady consumed with anger, rebellion, and fear.

Right off the bat, she experienced being in the womb and felt a lot of fear, hurt, and rejection. In addition, she was aware of angry voices outside the womb. She felt she wasn't wanted. God revealed that her Mother was very young and her Father didn't care about her. He told her they had considered an abortion and, as a fetus, she was aware they were considering aborting her. God also revealed that her Father had raped her Mother, causing the pregnancy, and then had to marry her. She picked up through the umbilical cord that her mother didn't want a baby and she interpreted those feelings to mean they didn't want *her*.

When she felt pain in the womb, God told her the pain she felt was her *Mother's* pain because her Father was hitting her Mother. She asked God how she could be healed of the hurt, fear, and pain.

"BY LETTING ME HEAL YOU."

At that point, I asked Anne to visualize Jesus. After a moment or two, she said He was up on a mountain where she had hiked. She walked up to were He was.

"Lord, can I put all these hurts, fears and pains in a sack and give them to You?
"THAT'S WHAT I WANT YOU TO DO."

She took some time to dump all her hurts, fears and pains into a garbage bag then gave the bag to Him. He put it on His back and said He was taking them so they couldn't ruin her life anymore. "Lord, what if these feelings come back?" He told her to remember she had given them to Him on the hill. He said if they returned, at that point she should tell Satan he could no longer hurt her, that he couldn't use these feelings against her and make her do bad things anymore.

She was sitting on the hill and she felt freer than when she first walked up to Him. As she looked up the mountain, she saw she still had a long way to go.

"Lord, was I with You before I was conceived?"
"YES."
"Did You create me for a purpose?"
"YES."

When she asked if He would reveal that purpose to her, He said He would *not* because she had some more things to go through first.

She asked God if she had been carrying around a lot of anger. He said that she had been because she thought what happened to her in her childhood was her fault and she had turned the hurt into anger. "Lord, have I been carrying around anger toward You?" He said that she had been because men had always hurt her. She knew He was the son of God and, since He was a man, she thought He had hurt her too. She

asked how she could get rid of this anger. He told her to go
back to the mountain and give it to Him. When she did, He
also put that on His back.

"Lord, what is this weird feeling?"
**"YOU ARE FEELING CLOSER TO ME. I WANT
TO ASSURE YOU THAT YOU WILL BE ABLE
TO GO THROUGH THESE SESSIONS AND IT
WILL BE ALL RIGHT. I WILL CALM YOUR
SPIRIT FOR YOU SO YOU CAN FREELY
MOVE THROUGH WHAT I HAVE TO SHOW
YOU."**

At the end of the session, She asked that, if this had been
from Jesus, He let her feel His peace. In her mind, she saw
herself sitting by a stream and feeling very calm. It was fall,
and the wind was blowing through the trees. She asked Jesus
what that place was. He told her it was a place made up in
her mind that He had created for her so that, when bad feelings come, she can retreat there and be with Him in her mind.
Jesus ended by assuring her that she would be healed.

When Anne came the second day, God indicated He
wanted her to start with her early childhood. He showed her
that when she was two, she and her baby brother were left at
a brick house that was not well-kept and trashy-looking. Her
Mother and Father were leaving. Her Mother told her she
would be back in a little while. An older lady picked up her
little brother and Anne followed them into the house. There
were a lot of other people there; teen-agers and smaller children, and all were bigger than she. Everyone seemed to be
doing their own thing, and Anne felt all alone.

That night, when she was put to bed, she asked the lady
when her Mother was coming back, but the lady didn't answer
her. Two weeks later, another lady was there. She was kind
of heavy and had long blonde hair. The older woman was

signing some papers and the blonde lady told Anne to go get in her car to go somewhere with her. Anne was confused. She didn't know where her brother was, and he was so small.

She was taken to another house. This was a big house. They went in the house, and the blonde lady talked with the people there. The people told Anne that she was going to stay there for awhile. Anne asked the blonde lady where her Mother was, and she said she didn't know. She left Anne with the man and woman. After a short stay there, it was time for her to move again. At this point, she was about three.

Anne got in the car with the blonde lady again and went to a big brick house. A woman with red hair and a man with red hair and a moustache and a boy with black hair came out. They told her she was to stay there for awhile. They went inside and had a birthday party for her with a chocolate cake. She stayed with them for a long time. They were good to her and she remembered a Christmas when they gave her things. They told her they were going to keep her with them. The blonde lady came back and after they talked with her, she left.

After being there for some time, Anne was told that they had to take care of an older woman and couldn't keep her any longer. Here came the blonde lady again, and Anne knew it was time to leave.

Now she was at another house with a Mama and four children. There, she shared a bedroom with the youngest girl, who was older than she. There was a big teddy bear there. She didn't have any toys of her own. One of the children, Bill, was 17 or 18. He liked her and took her to ride on his motorcycle and gave her a blue helmet that he told her would always be her own. When they got back from the ride, Bill was supposed to give her a bath. He started acting real weird. He had never acted like that before, but he said it was alright. He told her that all guys treated their little sisters like that. He was touching her real funny. It made her feel bad. He kept telling her she couldn't tell anybody. It was just their secret- between them. He told her that if she told anyone, he wouldn't take her places anymore and he wouldn't love her. Then, she was back on the bike with him again and there was this big pile of hay and he was doing it again. And then they left and went home.

The blonde lady came again and this time there were two other people with her- they were her Mom and Dad, but they weren't her Mom and Dad yet. She liked the lady because there was a cemetery across the street and she took her walking there. They came back often and took her places. Now it was a later time and the couple told her she was going to come and live with them forever.

They took her to a house that was painted green where there was a lot of room to run around and play, and a creek behind the house big enough for her to swim in. There was another old woman there and Anne liked her, and there was a funny-talking man. There was also a lady there with red hair. The old lady said she was her Grandma. And the funny-talking man was her Granddad. And the red-haired lady was her great aunt, because she was her Mom's aunt.

One day, her Mom and Dad got into their car and told her they were going to find and adopt her brother too. When they come back with a little boy, she said, "That's not my brother! My brother is a baby." But, they told her he was her brother, grown up some. She thought he was funny-looking, kind of chubby. They called it baby fat. And he was dirty, because he had been running around barefooted.

At that point, she returned to the scene in the bathroom with Bill. He was starting to act funny. (I asked her to visualize Jesus.) She saw Jesus right there, holding her. She said she knew what Bill was doing was not right because Jesus told her it wasn't right. He also told her that Bill was sick.

"Jesus, he doesn't look sick. Why doesn't he *look* sick?"

"BECAUSE HE IS SICK IN HIS MIND. SOMETHING LIKE THIS HAPPENED TO BILL WHEN HE WAS LITTLE. HE THOUGHT THAT WAS WHAT HE WAS SUPPOSED TO DO. HE WANTS YOU TO FORGIVE HIM BECAUSE HE KNOWS HE MADE YOU FEEL DIRTY."

"Lord, I forgive him. Can I forgive him and still be mad at him?"

"NO. YOU ARE SUPPOSED TO FEEL COMPASSION FOR HIM. THAT'S WHAT FORGIVING IS."

"Lord, how do You know he wants me to forgive him?

"WHETHER HE WANTS YOU TO FORGIVE HIM OR NOT IS NOT THE ISSUE HERE. THE IMPORTANT REASON YOU SHOULD FORGIVE HIM IS BECAUSE IT'S WHAT THE BIBLE SAYS YOU SHOULD DO. THE WAY YOU FORGIVE HIM IS IN YOUR HEART. YOU LET GOD TAKE CARE OF ALL THAT WENT ON AND CLEAN IT UP SO THAT IT DOESN'T HURT YOU SO BAD ANYMORE. WHEN YOU DO THAT, YOU WON'T BE ANGRY WITH HIM ANYMORE."

"Lord, could you clean it up now?"

"YES

Suddenly she was back in the special place that Jesus had prepared for her. She said it was like watching it on a big screen T. V. and now, it didn't hurt, and she felt calmer.

The next scene was a time when Anne's family moved and she had to make new friends, but she was shy and scared of meeting new people. She didn't like the way people treated her at her new school. She got mad with her Mom because after she told her Mom to take her out of that school because the people there didn't like her, her Mom wouldn't do it. Anne told her that if she didn't take her out of that school, she was going to kill herself like some girls she had seen on T. V. She asked for the keys to the car, and her Mom wouldn't give them to her, so she told her if she didn't give her the keys, she would take a knife and kill herself. In the next scene, she was in a hospital.

"God, why did I act so violently with my Mom?"
"YOU HAD TOLD A LOT OF LIES TO THE KIDS AT SCHOOL TO TRY TO GET THEM TO ACCEPT YOU, AND YOU DIDN'T THINK THEY LIKED YOU. THAT WASN'T REALLY YOU, IT WAS SATAN. HE WAS TRYING TO USE YOU TO DO SOMETHING REALLY BAD."
"How did Satan get such a hold on my life?"
"BECAUSE YOU WERE FEELING REJECTED AND YOU WERE SO DESPERATE FOR FRIENDS, YOU WERE WILLING TO DO ANYTHING, AND HE KNEW THAT."

I asked Anne to visualize Jesus in the scene with her mother. She said, "I can see Him in Mom. That's the reason I couldn't kill myself. I ran to a chair and got behind it. I put the knife to my chest, but He didn't let me cut myself. He didn't forcefully stop me either. He was holding me again.

"Lord, what was wrong with me?"
"YOU WERE SCARED TO GET CLOSE TO PEOPLE AND IT IS AT THIS POINT THAT YOU REALIZED YOUR REAL MOM WAS NOT COMING BACK. YOU FELT THAT IF

**YOU LOVE THESE PEOPLE YOU ARE WITH
NOW, YOU WOULD BE TURNING ON HER."**

She said, "Lord, if I love these people, am I really
turning on my mother?" Jesus told her this feeling was a lie
from Satan. Satan didn't want her to get close to people and
he was using her weakest spot against her. She then asked,
"Lord, can You bring healing for this feeling that I can't let
people get close to me?" God told her that He would, but that
it didn't happen at this point in her life, but later. She then
asked if it had happened for her now, at 17. Jesus gave her
a **"YES."**

Now, she was back in the hospital room and said that
since she didn't see the blonde lady, she must not be going to
another home. Her Mom and Dad have told her they would
come back the next day, but she didn't believe them. She felt
numb. She thought to herself, "I just don't care anymore."

"Lord, is it true that I just don't care any more?
**"NO. THAT FEELING IS JUST A WAY TO HIDE
THE HURT.**
"Then, the truth is, I care a lot?
**"YES. IT'S GOING TO BE OKAY. THEY ARE
GOING TO COME BACK.**

Now, it was a later time, and the hospital was checking
her vital signs. A man she described as "goofy" came in. He
told her he was the doctor. She told the goofy doctor that she
didn't want to go home, so he stuck her in a little room with
a cold floor and the walls had carpet on them.

"Lord, why did he put me in here?"
**"HE DIDN'T KNOW WHAT TO DO. YOU HAVE
BEEN HERE A LONG TIME AND HAVE MADE
NO PROGRESS. HE IS FRUSTRATED."**

"Lord, why haven't I made progress?"
"SATAN HAS THIS BIG WALL AROUND YOU AND YOU ARE TOO SCARED TO LET IT DOWN. DON'T WORRY THOUGH BECAUSE IT EVENTUALLY TURNS OUT OKAY."

The scene then shifted to a later time, and she was going home. She was happy she was out of that place. Suddenly, she was back in the special place Jesus had created for her. She asked, "Lord, what's happening here? I'm just sitting in my little place.

"Are You bringing healing to me here?"
"YES. I HAVE BROUGHT YOU HERE SO YOU CAN FEEL CALM ABOUT HOW YOUR LIFE HAS BEEN UP TO NOW."
"Lord, is this was a good time to stop for this session?"
"YES."

In her third session, God showed her a scene when she was in seventh grade. Her teacher met her in the hall and told her she was doing so well in school she could be moved to just one step below Honors. It had made her feel really good.
Then, Jesus showed her that her grades started coming down.

"Lord, why did that happen?"
"BECAUSE OF THE PEOPLE YOU WERE HANGING AROUND WITH. THEY DIDN'T LIKE SMART KIDS."
"Why was I drawn to them, Lord?"
"YOU HAD BEEN SO REJECTED BY NICE KIDS THAT YOU THOUGHT THEY WERE

THE ONLY KIDS WHO WOULD ACCEPT YOU."

He went on to tell her that this wasn't true, but that it was the way she perceived it. God then showed her that when she was in the eighth grade, she had some good friends, but at the same time, she felt rejected because, when they did things on the weekends, they didn't invite her. God said they didn't invite her because she lied a lot.

"Lord, why did I lie so much?"
"BECAUSE WHEN YOU CAME CLOSE TO GETTING CLOSE TO ANYBODY, OR CAME CLOSE TO LETTING THEM GET CLOSE TO YOU, YOU ACTED LIKE YOU WERE A TOUGH PERSON THAT THEY WOULDN'T WANT TO GET TO KNOW THAT WELL."

He showed her that she started hanging around with a rough crowd. Once she and a friend decided to skip school and run away from home, but they were caught before they could get out of town. God said He was showing her that because she needed to know her parents accepted her back even after that.

On a school holiday, when she was in the ninth grade, Anne and a bunch of kids decided to steal some champagne and get drunk. They stole the champagne and ran to the woods behind their house and started drinking. She got drunk. A 21-year-old friend took advantage of the situation and took her further back in the woods. God showed her that suddenly, he was all over her. He raped her. Afterwards, he told her that she was bleeding. She hurt real bad. It was all she could do to walk home. She immediately went up to her room and found that her pants were covered with blood. Her Mother came up to her room and saw them and that Anne had been drinking.

She pushed her down on a couch and tried to make her drink some water. When she wouldn't, she threw it in her face and said, "I know how to handle drunks!"

Later, an adult friend took Anne to the rape crisis center. Anne's head hurt. Her Mom was there with them and was real angry with Anne. After going through all the procedures at the hospital, Anne went back home and passed out for good. The next morning, she couldn't walk and her head hurt, and she literally had to crawl downstairs. It was a horrible week. She didn't tell the police what had happened.

"Lord, what kept me from telling them what happened?"
"YOU WERE DEFYING YOUR PARENTS."
"Why was I doing that, Lord?"
"YOU FELT BAD BECAUSE YOU COULDN'T GET GOOD FRIENDS. YOU SAID YOU WOULDN'T LET ANYTHING LIKE THAT HAPPEN TO YOU BECAUSE THAT IS WHAT HAPPENED TO YOUR BIRTH MOTHER."
"Lord, are You saying she got drunk and was raped, and that was how I was conceived?"
"YES, AND I'M SHOWING YOU THAT BECAUSE YOU NEED TO KNOW WHY YOU FELT SO MUCH ANGER FROM YOUR BIRTH MOM AND DAD."

Now, Anne was back at the place Jesus had prepared for her. She was packing a lot of stuff into a backpack and giving it to Jesus. It was like all this stuff was running back and forth in front of her face. Jesus told her that day in the woods, He let her pass out so she wouldn't have to feel the things the man did to her. Jesus told her He was holding her hand all the way through it.

Anne was just sitting there now, feeling empty. She asked Jesus what the empty feeling was. He said, **"IT'S BECAUSE YOU HAVE LEARNED SOME THINGS TODAY YOU DIDN'T KNOW. IT'S LIKE THEY ARE BEING SUCKED AWAY FROM YOU. ALL THE PAIN AND HURT IS BEING SUCKED OUT."** Anne asked if the empty space that was left could be filled by the Holy Spirit, and Jesus said it would be. She asked Jesus to let her feel His peace and immediately she did, there in the place He had created for her.

When we started the next day, Anne asked Jesus why she was feeling so sick. He told her she was overtired and that she didn't want to come to therapy that day. He said the reason she didn't want to come was because He wanted her to deal with her Father. She asked what Jesus wanted her to look at about her Father. **"HE HAS CAUSED SO MUCH FEAR IN YOU AND YOU'VE CARRIED THIS FEAR ALL YOUR LIFE."** That fear started when she was in the womb. When she was in the womb, her Father was angry a lot; he hit her Mother, and Anne thought he was hitting *her*, and she knew he didn't like her.

"Did I pick up on my Mother's feelings?"
"YES. YOU DIDN'T KNOW WHAT WAS GOING ON."
"Was my fear based on a lie?"
"SOME OF IT."
"Did any of my fear start at my birth?"
"YES. YOUR FATHER WASN'T THERE.

Jesus went on to explain that his not being there caused fear in her Mother. When he didn't show up, her Mother was afraid she was going to have to raise Anne all by herself. Jesus said her Mother was 15 when she had Anne.

Anne asked, "How did that fear affect me at birth, Lord?" **"IT MADE YOU FEEL HE WOULD NEVER BE THERE."** She then asked, "Did he also make me afraid after I was born?" The answer was he did. She asked Jesus to show her the first time he abused her. "I'm crying and I'm a baby and he's hitting me because I won't stop crying. He's yelling at me."

I asked her to visualize Jesus again.. "He's sitting there. He's comforting me."

"Lord, why didn't You make him stop?"
"BECAUSE HE IS NOT A PUPPET, AND HE HAD A CHOICE. HE DIDN'T LISTEN."

"Now, he's yelling at my Mother, telling her he didn't want to hear me crying anymore, and, if I wake him up again, he's going to do it worse. He doesn't like me. Now, he is hitting my Mother. He doesn't like either of us.

"Lord, what can I do?"
"YOU CAN'T STOP HIM."
"How can I survive this?"
"ONE DAY, YOU WILL BE ABLE TO HELP OTHER PEOPLE DEAL WITH THIS. BE STRONG."
"But, Lord, I'm just a baby!"
"I AM GOING TO HELP YOU. I WILL WALK YOU THROUGH THIS. EVERY TIME SOMETHING HAPPENS, I WILL BE RIGHT THERE."

Anne said she was crawling on the floor and her Father kicked her because she knocked something over. He started hitting her and her Mother tried to get him to stop, and he hit her Mother real hard.

"Lord, what is the message I should be getting out of this?"

"YOU HAVE TO GET OVER YOUR FEARS."

The scene changed and Anne was older now and walking. She was about 18 months old and her mom had a big belly. Anne was sitting in a chair and dropped something. Her Father picked her up and started hitting her. Then he put her on a table, a real tall place to her. He told her this was what she would get whenever she dropped something, and pushed her off the table. The fall hurt a lot, and there on the floor, he continued to hit her.

Once, when she was hungry, he wouldn't let her have anything to eat. That time, she hadn't done anything, but he hit her anyway. Then he got out a big belt and hit her real hard with it, and wouldn't stop.

"Lord, is there any message I'm supposed to get out of this?"

"YOU FEEL THAT NOBODY CARES. YOU FEEL YOU CAN'T DO ANYTHING RIGHT."

"Lord, are both of these lies?"

"YES, BUT YOU DIDN'T KNOW IT AT THE TIME."

"How has all this affected my life?"

"IT HAS MADE YOU REAL SHY AROUND PEOPLE YOU DON'T KNOW, AND YOU DON'T TRUST MEN."

"Did I buy the lie that I couldn't do anything right?"

"NO, BECAUSE YOUR MOTHER TOLD YOU THAT YOU COULD DO STUFF RIGHT. SHE TOLD YOU THAT ONE DAY, YOU WOULDN'T HAVE TO FACE HIM ANYMORE."

Anne said that now they were getting into a car, and her Mother told her they had to go to her Grandmother's house.

"Lord did my mother really love me?

"YES. SHE TOOK YOU TO YOUR GRANDMOTHER'S SO YOU WOULDN'T HAVE TO FACE WHAT YOUR FATHER WAS DOING TO YOU ANYMORE, BUT SHE COULDN'T TELL YOU WHAT SHE WAS DOING BECAUSE YOU WOULDN'T HAVE UNDERSTOOD."

"Why did Mother and my grandma get into such a fuss when we got there?"

"BECAUSE YOUR GRANDMOTHER HAD A LOT OF OTHER CHILDREN AND COULDN'T TAKE CARE OF ANYMORE BECAUSE YOUR MOTHER WAS THE OLDEST CHILD THAT SHE HAD."

"Lord, how can I be healed of the effects of the things my Father did to me?"

"YOU HAVE TO FACE UP TO YOUR FEAR OF HEIGHTS AND YOU NEED TO FORGIVE HIM."

"Lord, would You explain why he did those things to me?"

"HE WAS BEATEN AS A CHILD AND HE WAS ANGRY BECAUSE HE FELT HIS LIFE HAD BEEN RUINED AND HE TOOK IT OUT ON YOU."

Anne said now she was at her special place and was handing these things over to God and He was telling her that everything was going to be alright. She asked, "Lord, what is this empty feeling?' He said, **"IT IS LETTING GO A LOAD YOU HAVE CARRIED FOR 17 YEARS."** Then she asked why she was feeling so sad. Jesus told her it was because she had never let herself feel sad about it before. When she asked why she was feeling this, Jesus said it was a feeling of relief. He told her she would see her Mother again and it was going to be alright, but she wouldn't see her Father again.

She asked Jesus if He would fill the empty space inside with His Holy Spirit. He said He would and now, she didn't have to be afraid of heights.

"Lord, what do I do if I get to a high place and the fear comes?"
"JUST REMEMBER THAT THERE IS NOTHING TO BE AFRAID OF AND I WILL ALWAYS BE RIGHT THERE WITH YOU."
"Lord, can I talk with You like this all the time?"
"YES."

When we started that afternoon, Anne asked Jesus where He wanted her to start. He told her He wanted her to forgive her Father. She asked how she could do that. He told her she had to give up her hatred and anger toward him and give it to Him. She asked if she could put it all in a big sack and give it to Him. He said she could, and, after she did, she said it didn't hurt so bad anymore.

God then showed her He had given her the gift of helping other people, but until she got closer to Him, and let Him help her with it, she wouldn't know how to do it. Although she had the desire to be of help, she would only be able to use the gift with His help. Jesus reminded her of times she had tried to be of help- like the time one friend was in the hospital and she went to see him as often as she could, and another time when another friend had been hurting, and she had tried to help him through the pain he was feeling. Jesus told her the reason those situations had always turned out badly was because she hadn't known how to use the gift, and Satan used those situations to bring her down. He told her she had been carrying more pain at that point in her life than a 14-year-old girl could possibly deal with.

She said she was now in her special place just sitting there, and she was feeling very peaceful.

"Lord, are you ready now to tell me what my purpose is?"

"YES, TO BE A CHRISTIAN PSYCHOLOGIST. THROUGH THIS AREA YOU WILL HELP PEOPLE WITH THEIR HARD TIMES. YOU WON'T BE THE KIND WHO WILL DO IT FROM THE PSYCHOLOGICAL POINT OF VIEW, BUT FROM THE CHRISTIAN POINT OF VIEW. YOU WILL REACH THEM THROUGH THE SPIRITUAL PART."

She asked if there was anything she needed to do to start preparing herself for this. He told her she needed to change her ways and have more trust and faith. He said she could do this by keeping her eyes on Him.

She asked if she would be able to help many people. He said she would as long as she didn't let the world interfere. He said there would be a lot of things trying to turn her around, but she had to be strong and keep going. He also told her that many people enter this work for the money but very few have a gift like the one He had given her. He said that hers was a very strong gift which could be used for evil as well as for good and that was the reason Satan would come against her. He said He would not have given her this gift if she hadn't been strong enough to use it correctly.

She asked if she was stronger than she had realized she was. Jesus told her she was and, in her subconscious, she had always known that. That was the reason she had made it as far as she had. She said she felt different now, and Jesus told her what she was feeling was the Holy Spirit.

Now, she was back in her special place and she said she had never felt that calm before. It was like everything that had ever happened to her didn't hurt her the way it used to.

"IT'S OVER. THAT HURT AND PAIN IS OVER. IT CAN'T RULE YOUR LIFE ANYMORE.

She asked if she and I were through now. Jesus said that we weren't and that He wanted to close it all up in our next session.

When Anne came for our final day together in this group of sessions, she had recorded two dreams. She asked God if He had a message for her in the dreams. When He told her He did, she asked Him to help her interpret the meaning of the dreams. We took one dream at a time. We first made a list of each item in the dream. Then, taking these one by one, we asked Him if that item was symbolic of anything. If His answer was yes, we asked Him to tell us what it symbolized. After He had revealed to us what each item in the dream symbolized, we then asked Him to summarize in one or two sentences His message for her in the dream. We are only giving His final summary here.

The meaning of the first dream was that she would someday search for her birth mother and would find her, but she should not expect it to be like reunions she had seen in movies. He told her to rely on her adoptive parents because they would always be there for her.

God told her the meaning of the second dream was that she would meet a guy and they would become friends, and he would be the one God wanted her to be with, but first she had to do some growing. He told her she would have to learn how to let her guard down with guys, but that she should still be cautious.

"Lord, what else do You want to show me?"
"I WANT YOU TO REMEMBER THAT YOU CAN ALWAYS TALK WITH ME LIKE THIS, AND I WANT YOU TO REMEMBER EVERYTHING YOU HAVE LEARNED. I WANT YOU TO REMEMBER THAT EVERY-THING WILL HAPPEN IN MY TIME. DON'T TRY TO RUSH THEM."

She was back in her special place. Jesus was patting her on the back. She took that to mean she had done a good job. To be sure, she asked Him if He was pleased with her. He said He was.

She got up and picked up a cross that had been lying there and walked after Him down a road. She came to another road. She got off the road she had been on and got on the new road. She asked if it would be helpful for her to know what these two roads were

"THE ONE YOU CAME OFF OF WAS YOUR PAIN AND HURT. NOW YOU CAN GO ON THE ONE I WANT YOU ON."
"Why wasn't the cross I picked up any heavier than it was?"
"BECAUSE I ONLY GIVE YOU AS MUCH AS YOU CAN CARRY AND ALL THOSE BURDENS YOU HAVE BEEN CARRYING AREN'T ON YOU ANYMORE."

At that point, Jesus told her that her work here was completed for now.

But that wasn't the end of Anne's story.

After she was here in April of 1991, I didn't hear anything from Anne for about seven years. Not hearing from a client after they receive healing is normal. We usually don't know what happens in a person's life after they come for healing, especially if they are not from this general area, as was the case with Anne. We don't do follow-ups, knowing it's God's responsibility to see to their continued healing.

Anne made an appointment to come back, and this time she brought her husband with her. When she came, she was terribly distraught. She was crying and almost beside herself with grief. She had searched for her birth family and located them in a neighboring state. When she went to see her birth mother, she found her mother had Huntington's Chorea and that Huntington's ran in the family.

Huntington's Chorea is a rare, inherited degenerative disease that occurs in mid-life and progresses to dementia. Chorea literally means "dance," and is descriptive of the jerky movements occurring in people who have the disease. Symptoms seldom occur before marriage and childbearing. There is no treatment for the disease and also nothing to control its symptoms.

Anne went on to tell me that the process for determining if a person has inherited Huntington's is complicated and takes time for the results to be analysed. She had had the tests done, but did not expect to hear back from them for several weeks. In the meantime, she was frightened to death that she would be affected, along with her child, and any other children she might have.

In the process of talking with God, she was told that her fear and anger had separated her from Him, and that this fear had been a lifelong problem for her. He said her fear and anger were caused by an ancestral bond that went back on her birth mother's side for three generations, caused by abuse and witchcraft. He said Anne didn't need to know the specifics about this. He wanted to heal her family of the abuse and witchcraft. She asked what she needed to do in order to be healed. The answer was **"PRAYER AND FAITH."** When she asked Him to start the healing on her mother's side, He said that he would, with her.

The ancestral bond on her birth father's side also went back three generations. These bonds were caused by anger, resentment, and abuse. God told her He was also healing her of the effects of her father's side.

He said that He had brought her and her brother out of her birth family and put them in a family which had His light so that they could shine and be the way out of darkness for others.

She asked, "What about the Huntington's?" He told Huntington's was irrelevant because she and her brother had *not* been brought out of their birth family with Huntington's. He assured her that her son would not be affected nor would any other children she might have. After He revealed this to her, her relief was immediate. She obviously felt His peace, which passes understanding. She headed home, believing what God had revealed to her.

Several weeks later, I got a phone call from a joyous Anne. The results of the tests had come back and she had been assured that she did not have Huntington's, and would not be passing it down to her children.

Anne did get her degree in psychology, as God had directed. She has been given a special talent to help hurting people.

17.

Omega-
Martha's Healing

Martha came to us in February, 2001 and was set free from the things that had bound her five years later, in February, 2006.

Although she had been a Christian for most of her life, she was bound by many demons due to having grown up in an extremely dysfunctional family. Among the emotions we dealt with over that five year period were:

Fear- of rejection, of speaking, of making mistakes,
of failure, of the unknown, of ridicule
Insecurity- lack of esteem, hopelessness, helplessness,
distrust, doubt, self-doubt, loneliness, helplessness
Guilt
Anger- bitterness, resentment, frustration

At one point in her Christian walk, Martha had felt a call from God to preach, but nothing had come from that. In the meantime, she had been very active in her church. She volunteered for any job that came along. She wanted very much to be helpful. She had taken on so many things by the time she came to us that she had burned herself out. In addition to her work at church, she was home-schooling her children and, when she first came, also had a job outside her home.

In our very first session, after God had told her she needed healing, she asked, "What will it take in order for me to be healed?" God's answer was, **"TO GET OVER YOUR FEAR OF REJECTION."** It's interesting that, after we worked through all the things listed above, we came back to the basic problem of her fear of rejection and at that point, Jesus healed her and set her free.

In the first session, God told her He had created her for a purpose, that He had a perfect plan for her. He also told her one of her problems was guilt, but because Jesus had died for her, He didn't hold her guilty for anything. Her problem was, she held *herself* guilty.

At the end of that first session, She asked, "Lord, what is my next step?" He said, **"JUST WAIT ON ME."** She waited on Him for almost five years.

Jesus communicates with people in different ways- in words, in visions, in feelings, in dreams. He communicated to Martha in all those ways.

In many of our sessions, we dealt with current problems going on in Martha's life. In addition to her own children, she was raising her brother's children. At rare times he would pay child support, but most of the time, he wouldn't.

Over the five years, Jesus continued to tell Martha to "rest." In a vision in one of the early sessions, He and she were together and they disappeared into a bright light. She felt at peace and that she was in the place where she was supposed to be. Jesus told her this was a healing He was taking her through. There was no one else there. One of her ongoing problems was her concern about what others might think or say. She asked Jesus if she could come back to this place with Him when she became concerned about what others were thinking or saying.

"WHY DO YOU HAVE TO LEAVE? YOU CAN STAY HERE AS LONG AS YOU LIKE."

At another time, He told her, **"I WANT YOU TO HAVE PEACE IN THE MIDST OF WHAT IS GOING ON. YOU CAN DO THAT BY FOCUSING ON ME. DON'T ALLOW THE CIRCUMSTANCES AROUND YOU TO KEEP YOU FROM FOCUSING ON ME."**

"Lord, are You saying You want me to learn to deal with stress when I am in the middle of stress?"
"LEARN TO RELAX. YOU PUT TOO MUCH PRESSURE ON YOURSELF TRYING TO BE PERFECT. YOU TRY TO DO EVERYTHING RIGHT FOR OTHERS."
"Do I do that so I will be accepted?"
"NO. SO THAT YOU WILL *FEEL* ACCEPTED."

He went on to tell her that when she was growing up, her father had always expected more from her than she was able to give. He was never satisfied with anything she did.

2001 Sessions

In our session on June 16, she asked Jesus about a vision she had when she was praying in church. She had a pile of junk and she was adding to it. Jesus came over and put all the junk in a duffle bag and carried it off. In the next scene, He was standing beside a table and the junk was all spread out on the table. He seemed to just be piddling with all the things. She asked what the message was that she was supposed to be getting out of this.

"IT IS NOT JUNK TO ME."
"What is it to You, Lord?"
"IT'S THINGS I CAN FIX. THE MORE JUNK YOU GIVE ME, THE MORE I CAN USE."
"Do You want me to bring You all my junk?"
"YES. AND THERE IS MORE JUNK TO BRING."
"What kind of junk do I still need to bring?"
"INSECURITIES, FEAR. LIES FROM THE DEVIL."
"Lord, can You help me bring these to You?"

At that point, He seemed to be trying to take something away from her. She asked what that was she didn't want to let go. He said, **"CONTROL. CONTROLLING. YOU ARE AFRAID TO LOSE CONTROL."**

On June 23, she asked God why she felt out of place. He said it was a feeling she had had for a long time- going back to before she was born. He said that when her mother found she was pregnant, she felt it was an inconvenient time to be having a baby. That made her mother fearful. It had also been her Father's feeling and she picked up on their feelings through the umbilical cord. She asked Jesus if this was the reason she had always felt she was an inconvenience. He said it was and it was also the reason she wanted to withdraw from time to time. He told her she had never been an inconvenience and that it was a lie directly from the devil. When she asked if she could bind this feeling and cast it out in His name, He said she could but He also wanted her to walk through it. She asked Him to explain that.

"WHEN YOU FEEL THOSE TIMES OF BEING OUT OF PLACE, RECOGNIZE WHERE IT

CAME FROM, AND GO ON THROUGH IT ANYWAY."

He ended the session by saying, **"YOU ARE NOT AN INCONVENIENCE TO ME."**

On June 28, she asked Jesus if He could help her with the rejection she had been feeling at work. He told her that He could and that she should walk through it.

"THIS HAS BEEN A PART OF YOUR LIFE FOR SO LONG, YOU HAVE TO LEARN TO WALK THROUGH IT."
"Jesus, are You in the process of healing me of the feeling of rejection?"
"NO. I HAVE HEALED YOU OF THE REJECTION, BUT IT IS THE SYMPTOMS THAT I HAVE TO WALK YOU THROUGH."

A little later, she and Jesus were walking and she found there were some things dragging in the dirt behind her. She asked Him what they were. He said, **"SYMPTOMS AND FEELINGS."** She asked Him to untie those things so she wouldn't have to drag them around. He said He could, but He didn't think she really wanted Him to. When she asked why He thought she wouldn't want Him to, He said, **"I'M AFRAID IT WOULD BE TOO BIG A SHOCK TO YOU."** He went on to say that He had already started releasing the things and would continue to release them, one by one, as He thought she could handle it. He told her He wanted her to know what it would be like when all these things were released. She felt that now and started dancing down the road.

"Are You saying that in time, You will release all these things from my life?"

"YES. I'M GOING TO GIVE YOU THE DESIRES OF YOUR HEART."

On July 16, Jesus told her that she feared what other people thought. She asked what she could do about that.

"THERE IS NOTHING YOU CAN DO. NO ONE CAN CONTROL WHAT OTHER PEOPLE THINK, BUT YOU CAN CONTROL HOW IT MAKES YOU FEEL AS I HEAL YOU."

On August 14, Martha had a vision of Jesus coming down from His throne, and as He did, He got bigger and bigger. He told her He was demonstrating that He wanted to grow in her life.

She started feeling lonely. She asked if this was a burden she had carried. Jesus told her it was, and she had carried it since she was five. She asked what happened at five that started this feeling of loneliness. Jesus showed her a church her family had attended. She was there, holding her brother so she wouldn't be alone. There was a group of girls there, but Martha had the feeling she didn't fit in. She asked Jesus if it was the other girls that made her feel lonely, or if it was something in her. He told her it was something in her. He said she felt she didn't fit in with the girls there because in her family, she didn't fit in with her brothers. She felt that way with her brothers because she was always left behind. She asked if she had gotten the feeling that she didn't count. Jesus said that the feeling was she didn't *mean* anything. She also felt she didn't mean anything because she wasn't a boy.

On September 10, Martha asked, "Lord, how long have I had a problem with rejection?"

"FROM DAY ONE."
"Lord, is day one the day I was conceived?"
"YES."
"Did my mother want to get pregnant?"
"BAD TIMING. SHE WAS AFRAID TO HAVE A BABY AT THAT TIME. YOU PICKED UP ON YOUR MOTHER'S FEELING THROUGH THE CORD, AND IT MADE YOU FEEL INSECURE, UNWANTED AND REJECTED. YOUR FATHER ESPECIALLY DIDN'T WANT A BABY GIRL."

On November 7, Jesus said, **"I WANT TO RELEASE YOU FROM THE STRINGS THAT HAVE BEEN PUT ON YOU. THE STRINGS ARE THE OPINIONS OF OTHER PEOPLE."**

On November 28, Martha asked Jesus about a vision He had given her. In the vision, she was holding something in her hand that she was very careful with. She asked Jesus what she was carrying. He told her it was a gift and a talent He had given her. She handed the gift to Jesus and asked why she was giving it to Him. He took the gift in His hands and it seemed He wanted to talk with her about it. He seemed to be content or pleased that she had given it back to Him. He was smiling. He had been sitting on the edge of His chair, but then leaned back and put the gift on His lap. She asked if He was pleased with the way she had used the gift. He said, **"NO. I AM PLEASED WITH THE WAY YOU HAVE GIVEN IT BACK TO ME."** He went on to tell her that the gift was her life.

At that point, Martha was sitting on Jesus' lap. She was trying to figure it all out. She put her head on His shoulder. She asked Jesus to please make all that clear to her. He was wanting to reassure her. He referred her back to a time when she had displeased Him. At that point in her life, she had told

Him to give her calling to someone else. She said she had become oppressed with disobedience. She felt that because of her disobedience, she had broken their relationship. She asked if she was worthy of the gift.

"NO. EVERYONE SINS AND COMES SHORT OF THE GLORY OF GOD."
"Am I as worthy as anyone else?"
"YES."
"Lord, have You forgiven me for my disobedience?"
"I DID THAT A LONG TIME AGO."
"Do I have a hard time *accepting* Your forgiveness?"
"MY FORGIVENESS AND MY LOVE. YOU HAVE JUDGED YOURSELF MORE HARSHLY THAN I HAVE AND I WILL HELP YOU LEARN TO STOP NEGATIVELY JUDGING YOURSELF."

She kept seeing Him holding her. She was looking up at Him. He was talking to her and lovingly playing with her hair. The last thing He told her in this session was, **"I AM YOURS, AND YOU ARE MINE."**

On December 10, He told her He was teaching her to be sensitive to the Spirit.

2002 Sessions

On July 17, Jesus was embracing Martha, but it wasn't like it was *His* arms, but arms of fire wrapped around her.

"Lord, is this like a hedge of thorns to protect me?"
"NO. THE FIRE IS TO BURN OUT THE DOUBT THAT HAS PLAGUED YOUR LIFE."

"Lord, is there anything else You want to tell me about that?"
"JUST STAY IN THE FIRE."

On August 16, Martha said she felt she might be tying Jesus' hands, preventing Him from blessing her family the way He wanted to. He told her the problem was **"THE CURSE OF DOUBT."** She asked what she needed to do to get rid of the doubt.

"IT GOES BACK TO THE REST. I WILL GIVE YOU PERFECT PEACE IF YOUR MIND IS STAYED ON ME BECAUSE YOU TRUST ME."
"Lord, is doubt the dog I dreamed about recently that was attacking me?"
"THAT IS WHAT YOU HAVE BEEN FIGHTING AGAINST AND THE OTHER THINGS ARE ENTWINED AROUND IT. YOU HAVE DOUBTED ME BECAUSE YOU HAVE BEEN FIGHTING AGAINST THESE THINGS SO LONG."
"Lord, how can I keep financial and physical problems from influencing me?"
"GO BACK TO SITTING IN MY LAP."

2003 Sessions

On April 4, Jesus told her that her father had always compared her to her brothers and that gave her the drive to try to prove that she could do anything. When she had become aware of his watching her to see if she could do things, she started being afraid to try new things because of what her father would think if she failed.

In our session on May 20, Martha asked Jesus if His promises applied to her. He said, **"YES, IF YOU WILL LET THEM."** He said if she didn't think His promises applied to her, they wouldn't. When she asked how she could believe they applied to her, He said, **"FAITH."** She just needed to believe that they applied to her, and they would.

He said she needed to find out why it was so hard for her to believe. She said, "I remember when I was 15, I had planned to go to RN school, and Daddy told me I couldn't go because he didn't have the money. Lord, has this come from all the times I had planned something and it didn't work out?" Jesus said, **"YOUR DREAMS AS A CHILD DIDN'T WORK OUT."** This was the reason she was having trouble accepting what He was doing for her. She asked if her heart was sick because of what happened to her as a child. Jesus said, **"HOPE DEFERRED MAKES THE HEART SICK."** When she asked if this was the reason she was afraid to hope, Jesus said it was the reason she was afraid to *trust*. That was the reason she had always tried to take things into her own hands and was where the controlling spirit came from.

Jesus said that she had to come to a resting point somewhere. She asked Him to define "resting point."

"EITHER YOU BELIEVE WHAT I HAVE SAID I WOULD DO, OR YOU WON'T BELIEVE I WILL DO WHAT I HAVE SAID I WOULD DO."

Now, she was on an altar and was struggling to be still. When she asked Jesus if He would help her be still, He said, **"BE STILL AND KNOW THAT I AM GOD."** He ended the session by letting her know that she didn't have to do anything for Him to love her.

On June 26, Martha asked Jesus why much of the time she felt so unimportant to Him. He told her it had been programmed into her thinking. She asked if it would help her get reprogrammed if she quoted scripture to Satan. He said it would, and it would also help if she meditated on scripture.

On July 7, she asked Jesus if He could take away her feelings of loneliness; He said He didn't want to, because He wanted her to learn to walk through it.

2004 Sessions

On April 14, Jesus told her He wanted to talk to her about the word "believe." She asked, "Believe in what?" He said, **"BELIEVE IN ME."** He told her she only believed in him to a point, and that fear was the thing keeping her from fully believing in Him. When she asked where that fear was coming from, He told her all fear comes from Satan. When she asked Him to tell her specifically what she was afraid of, He told her she was afraid to trust Him. She asked if the reason she was afraid to trust Him was because she didn't trust herself. He said that her failing to trust herself made it impossible for her to trust Him, or anyone.

She asked Jesus to tell her what she could do to start trusting herself as she should.

"LOOK TO THE HILLS WHERE YOUR STRENGTH COMES FROM."
"Are You saying I need to focus more on You?"
"MORE ON MY STRENGTH."

He went on to tell her one of her major problems was trying too much to depend on herself.

Prior to our session on May 27, Martha had been praying that Jesus consume (the things in) her (which were keeping her from trusting Jesus). Prior to our session, Jesus had given her a vision of a lumber yard that was on fire. A part of her was wanting to get out of the lumber yard, and another part was pushing her in.

"Lord, how can I get rid of the things that you want to consume?"

"TRUST. THE FEAR IS TRYING TO GET YOU OUT OF THE LUMBER YARD BECAUSE FEAR DOESN'T WANT YOU TO BE CONSUMED."

"Lord, are You saying that You want me to be consumed?"

"I'M ANSWERING YOUR PRAYER THAT YOU BE CONSUMED."

"Lord, if I allow You to consume me, what will that mean?"

"THAT YOU GIVE UP YOUR DESIRES, DREAMS AND HOPES."

"And, what do I replace these with, Lord?

"WITH *MY* DESIRES, DREAMS AND HOPES."

"How do I do that, Lord?"

"TRUST."

"Is this our of my reach?"

"YES, BUT IT IS NOT OUT OF MY REACH AND I WANT YOU TO DEPEND ON MY REACH INSTEAD OF YOURS."

"Lord, what is my next step in getting to where You want me to be?"

"JUST KEEP DOING WHAT YOU HAVE BEEN DOING AND EVERYTHING WILL BE OKAY."

At one point in our session on June 17, Jesus said that Satan was attacking her unusually hard because she had reached a crossroad and he didn't want her to cross over. Jesus said Satan knew he couldn't defeat her, and was just trying to slow her down. Satan was trying so hard because she had been praying about generational curses in her family. Jesus confirmed there *were* several generational curses.

She said, "Jesus, I know You can break those curses. Would You do it right now? He said, **"I WANT YOU TO KNOW MORE ABOUT THEM. IF I BREAK THEM, YOU WON'T UNDERSTAND ABOUT THEM."** He told her a financial curse was one of them, and that the curse started with her mother and father. She said, "Lord, didn't their parents and their parents' parents struggle with the same thing?" Jesus said that they did, but it was through her parents that it affected her. Because of the financial curse, she had accepted the fact that life would always be hard financially. Jesus told her the curse had also come down through her husband's family.

"Lord, are You saying this financial curse came because I figured that was the way it was? **"YOU JUST ACCEPTED IT AND IT IS BASED ON A LIE."** "Jesus, I realize now that the financial curse has come because I have bought into a lie. Could You break the curse now?" **"YES. AND YOU CAN BREAK THE HOLD IT HAS ON YOU BY LOOKING AT THE LIGHT."**

On August 15, Martha had been talking with Jesus about her problem of not believing in herself. Jesus had just told her that this unbelief went back to her father, because her father didn't believe in her. She asked what it would take for all this unbelief to be removed. **"YOU HAVE TO**

FORGIVE YOUR FATHER AND YOUR BROTHERS."
Martha asked if she could just tell Him that she forgave them for all their doubting of her. **"JUST YOUR WANTING TO FORGIVE THEM IS ENOUGH."** "Lord, I do want to forgive them. Will that be enough?" He said that it was a start and when Martha asked if He meant that was a *start* of her healing, He said, **"YES."**

At the end of that session, when Martha asked if there was anything else, Jesus told her to hurry up, that she was running behind. When she asked why He said that, He said, **"I HAVE AN IMPORTANT JOB FOR YOU TO DO AND YOU CAN'T DO IT WITH ALL THIS NEGATIVE STUFF."**

2005 Sessions

There was one brother that Martha had an especially hard time forgiving because he had taken advantage of her numerous times and was in a position to continue to do so. In our session on January 13, Jesus told her again that she should forgive him.

> "Lord, I don't *want* to forgive him. If I forgive him, I would be allowing him to hurt me again."
> **"FORGIVE HIM FOR WHAT HE HAS DONE."**
> "If I do, will he hurt me again?"
> **"YES."**
> "Then, why should I want to forgive him?"
> **"BECAUSE I FORGAVE YOU."**
> "Lord, will you get me to the point where I can really forgive him?"
> **"THAT IS ALL I WANT. I JUST WANT YOU TO *CHOOSE* TO FORGIVE HIM."**

January 19

"STOP WORRYING ABOUT OTHERS' OPINIONS AND WORK THROUGH IT."
"Would You help me learn to do that?"
"I WANT TO."
"Lord, if You want to, what is keeping You from doing it?"
"THE DEVIL DOESN'T WANT YOU TO HAVE IT."
"Lord, what is this "it" You are talking about?"
"HE DOESN'T WANT YOU TO HAVE ANYTHING- HEALING, FORGIVENESS, SECURITY."
"Lord, are You saying he can prevent Your giving these things to me?"
"NO, BUT HE CAN KEEP YOU FROM RECEIVING THEM."
"How can he do that?"
"BY PLAYING GAMES, BY DISTRACTING YOU."
"Lord, do I believe that You have everything I need"
"YES."
"Then why do I believe You won't give me what I need?"
"BECAUSE YOUR DADDY NEVER DID."

February 2

"YOUR FEAR HAS CAUSED YOU TO FEEL ISOLATED. YOU ARE AFRAID YOU WILL DO THINGS WRONG AND BE LAUGHED AT."
"Lord, why do I feel so inferior to other people?"
"BECAUSE OF FINANCES. YOU WERE ALWAYS MUCH POORER THAN OTHERS.

219

YOU ALWAYS HAD TO HAVE THEIR HAND-ME-DOWNS."
"Lord, was my main concern that they would laugh at me if I did something wrong?"
"IT GOES BACK TO YOUR MOTHER. SHE FELT INFERIOR TO THEM AND THAT MADE YOU FEEL INFERIOR. YOU PICKED UP ON YOUR MOTHER'S FEELINGS. I WANT TO HEAL YOU OF YOUR FEELINGS OF INFERIORITY."

When our session started on February 17, Jesus told Martha that He wanted to start at the beginning. She saw herself in the womb and said she must have been happy because she was jumping in the womb. Her father came in, and he and her mother started quarreling. She became aware that her mother was upset and she was yelling at her father. She realized they were fussing about her, so she stopped jumping and drew back as far as she could. Her daddy was upset because her mother was pregnant. It had made Martha feel she was unwanted. After her father got so upset, her mother wished she was not pregnant and Martha picked up on that. Martha asked Jesus what effect all this had had on her life. He said, **"YOU HAVE NEVER KNOWN WHETHER YOU BELONGED."**

When Martha asked Jesus if He had a reason for sending her into that family, He said, **"YOU HAVE A PURPOSE AND A DESTINY."** He told her that through her, the curse of rejection could be broken in the family. She asked if He wanted the curse broken.

"DO YOU WANT THE CURSE BROKEN?"
"Lord, why would I *not* want the curse broken?"
"IF THE CURSE IS BROKEN, IT WILL OPEN UP A WHOLE NEW LIFE."

"Lord, are You saying I've gotten so used to the curse, it is a part of me?"

"YOU DON'T KNOW HOW TO LIVE YOUR LIFE WITHOUT IT."

"Is my fear of change a barrier to the curse being healed?"

"YES."

"Lord, I want to be healed, but I'm afraid. Could You tell me specifically what I'm afraid of?"

"YOU ARE AFRAID OF LOSING *YOU*."

When she had other questions about this, Jesus told her she wasn't ready for the change and she needed to be patient.

At the session on February 24, Jesus took Martha back to the time her mother had just told her father that she was pregnant. What happened back then had affected her security- she didn't feel valued by her parents and didn't feel secure in her relationship with them. It had affected the way she saw herself as an adult. Because she didn't feel valued by her family, she didn't feel valued by her church. She asked if she felt she had to do something to be valued. Jesus said she did, and when she asked if she felt she had always had to try to prove herself, Jesus said, **"YOU FEEL YOU CAN'T PROVE YOURSELF."** He went on to say that not being able to prove herself didn't stop her from trying, but it did lead to frustration.

There was a great deal of darkness in Martha's life. Many times, she would be seeing a vision and suddenly, everything would go dark. She asked, "Lord, why am I afraid the darkness will always win out?" Jesus said, **"BECAUSE YOU FEEL IT ALWAYS HAS, BUT THAT WILL END."** Jesus said the darkness had come into her through her father and the darkness was caused by idol worship. At the end of this session, Jesus told her that He had pulled the darkness out of her.

On March 9, when Martha asked Jesus what he wanted to show her next, He said, **"THE PROCESS THAT IS BEGINNING."** He told her to not be afraid of the process. He said she wasn't afraid of change, but she did fear the *process* of change. She was afraid of the process because she was afraid she would mess it up. When she asked if Satan was putting this fear in her, Jesus told her that she was fighting his doing it. She was afraid of giving Satan a way to reenter her life. He said He was trying to help her keep from giving Satan access. She asked Jesus if He was saying she was really free, but Satan was trying to make her believe she was not free. Jesus said **"YES,"** and told her that the best way to keep Satan from coming back was to concentrate on Him.

When Jesus asked what she was working for, she asked Him to tell her the answer. He said, **"APPROVAL."** She said, "Jesus, if I'm free, why am I working for approval?" He said it went back to the process He had just told her about. When she asked if He wanted her to be free from the need for approval, He said, **"YES, AND MANY MORE."** When she asked how to get rid of it, He told her it was going to be a process and that she would be freed over time.

There were other things He wanted to break in her life. He told her it wasn't Satan she would have to fight against as much as it was the old stuff that had been contaminated by the darkness. She asked Jesus if He could put all that stuff in a bag, tie it up and get rid of it. Jesus said that He could, but it would be a shock to her. He said there was a purpose in her going through the process, that she could learn more by going through the process than she could otherwise. When He asked if she was willing to go through the process, Martha said, "I have to, Lord; what choice do I have?" He said, **"YOU CAN EITHER ENJOY THE PROCESS OR DREAD THE PROCESS."**

She asked if there was anything else He wanted to tell her about that. Jesus said, **"NOT THAT YOU WANT TO HEAR."** She asked, "Why do You say that, Lord?" He said it was because her healing would take patience and commitment. She said, "Patience with myself, or with You?" He said, **"PATIENCE WITH ME."**

"Lord, what difference will it make in my life if I go with the Process?"
"IF YOU GO WITH THE PROCESS, IT IS LIKE WALKING IT OUT, AND YOU WILL WALK IT OUT WITH ME AND WITH MY ABUNDANT LIFE."
"What will happen if I don't go through the process?"
"ALL YOU HAVE BEEN THROUGH AND WORKED THROUGH UP TO THIS POINT WILL BE FOR NAUGHT."

She felt if she *didn't* go through the process she would have no need of Him, and Jesus told her that was true for everybody.

He assured Martha that, at the end of the process, she would be free. At the end of the session, Jesus said, **"COME UNTO ME ALL YE THAT ARE WEARY AND HEAVY LADEN, AND I WILL GIVE YOU REST."** Martha asked Jesus if He would give His rest to her. He said, **"IF YOU WILL STOP BEING A STUBBORN CHILD AND ACCEPT IT."**

On March 30, when Martha asked Jesus what she should be doing right then, He said, **"BE CONTENT."** She answered, "How can I be content when I'm so bored?" He told her it was not boredom, but the fact she felt she was supposed to be *doing* something. She said, "Jesus, are You telling me I should let go of control?" **"IF YOU WOULD DO THAT, YOU WOULD BE CONTENT."**

On April 14, Jesus told her if she was looking for healing, she was looking in the wrong direction. He said the evidence she was looking for wasn't the evidence she really wanted to see; and, in addition, she had been looking for acceptance by people when what she *should* be looking for was righteousness, peace, and joy in the Holy Spirit. He said Satan was playing a game, and she was allowing him to do that. She said, "Lord, what do You mean I'm allowing him to play the game?" He said, **"IT HAS TO DO WITH YOUR FEELINGS. YOU ARE ALLOWING YOUR FEELINGS TO RULE YOU."**

Later, when Martha asked Jesus how she could move truth from her head into her heart, He said she should meditate. She told Him it was a struggle for her to meditate and He said that was because Satan didn't want her to meditate. When she asked Jesus to help her learn to meditate without having to struggle so much, Jesus said, **"YOU NEED TO LEARN TO RELAX."** She said, "Lord, You tell me all these things to do- how do I find *time* to do them?" He told her to stop doing some other things; that she needed to stop reading all the time. She asked why He was saying that- she was only reading the Bible and Christian books. He said, **"STOP READING AND START THINKING."** He said her time should be balanced between reading books and allowing Him to teach her.

She said, "When I was a child, I spent a lot of time thinking about negative stuff. It became a pastime for me." She asked Jesus if that was a habit that had been hard for her to break. He told her that this was the reason she wouldn't allow herself to stop and think; she was afraid she would get back into the habit of negative thinking. He told her if she trusted Him to help her think and kept her eyes on Him, she wouldn't drift back into her old habit of negative thinking.

When Martha asked Jesus to sum up what He had been trying to tell her in that session, He said, **"MY STRENGTH HAS BEEN MADE PERFECT IN YOUR WEAKNESS, BUT YOU HAVE TO BE WILLING TO CALL ON MY STRENGTH."**

In our session on April 21, Martha said something like tennis balls were stuck all over her. Jesus told her the balls represented evil spirits. She saw Satan throwing those balls at her. She would get rid of one and another one would come right back. She asked Jesus why those things were sticking to her. He said it was because she had let her guard down and had allowed herself to get discouraged. The way to push those things away was to take back her courage. She said, "During the time when Jesus pulled the seed of darkness out of me, I felt we had gotten to the bottom of it, but it wasn't going to go away. That was when discouragement hit me. It made me think there wasn't going to be an end."

She asked Jesus if He had pulled all the darkness out of her. He told her the darkness was gone, but the *power* of the darkness, the effect it had had on her, was not gone. When she asked why the effect of the darkness didn't leave with the darkness, He told her it was too much a part of her. She said, "Lord, if the effects are still all there, what good did it do to remove the darkness?"

"IT CLOSES THE DOOR
"Lord, are You saying that You have healed me and I need to accept the healing?"
"I HAVE DELIVERED YOU, BUT I HAVEN'T HEALED YOU."
"Lord, what do I do with all this heaviness?"

225

"I'M TAKING IT OFF YOU AND PUTTING IT ON MYSELF. WHEN I DO, ALL THE BALLS WILL FALL OFF."

At this point, He took the heaviness off her. Martha was sitting down. Jesus was standing there, looking at her. He still had her heaviness on Him. She said, "Lord, can't You do something with that heaviness and get rid of it? He said, **"WHY?"** She said, "I want to be able to live my life without all that stuff. Isn't that enough of an answer? What should the right answer be, Lord? Why should I want to be made whole?" Jesus said, **"AS A TESTIMONY FOR WHAT I CAN DO."** She asked Jesus if her reason for wanting to be made whole had been a selfish one; He said that it had been.

She asked if He could let her feel His peace. He said He couldn't because she was too angry with Him. She asked Him to tell her why she was angry, and he said, **"BECAUSE YOU SEE THE DELAY AS DENIAL, YOU ARE NOT WILLING TO WAIT."** She said, "Lord, You know what a problem this is causing me. What can I do about it?" At this point, Jesus squatted down and started talking to her. She said she looked like a little child who couldn't have what she wanted, that she must be a stubborn-willed child. Now she didn't know what to do, so she asked Jesus what she should do. He told her that she had to make a choice. She said it was like the choice of whether she had Him. She wanted Him. But, did she want to have Him and stay where she was, to have life the way it was and not have it get any better- or did she want to have Him and go with Him and take a chance that things would get better? She said she didn't think she had the strength to go with Him.

She said, "Lord, You know how tired I am. Could You just let me rest in peace and let's talk about it some other time?" At that point, Jesus picked her up and held her and she knew at least for then, she didn't have to go anywhere.

April 27

"Lord, do I fear being healed?
"YOU ARE AFRAID TO *PURSUE* HEALING. YOU ARE AFRAID OF THE OUTCOME."
"Would You explain that?"
"HOPE DEFERRED MAKES THE HEART SICK. YOU ARE AFRAID TO HOPE BECAUSE YOU ARE AFRAID YOU WILL BE DISAPPOINTED. ARE YOU GOING TO PURSUE YOUR HEALING?"
"Lord, is there any reason *You* don't want me to pursue healing?"
"RIGHT NOW, YOU CAN'T HANDLE IT BECAUSE YOU ARE AFRAID IT WILL DESTROY YOU."
"Lord, can I do all things through You?"
"YES."
"Then, can I be healed by You"
"IF YOU PURSUE ME."
"Lord, haven't I been pursuing You?"
"YOU HAVE BEEN PURSUING *HEALING*."
"When You say I should pursue *You*, what do You mean, Lord?"
"YOUR HEALING WILL BE FOUND IN ME. YOU CAN'T SEPARATE YOUR HEALING FROM ME."
"Lord, how can I pursue You?"
"BY LETTING GO EVERYTHING BUT ME."
"Lord, what is the next step You want me to take to get to where You want me to be?"
"TRUST."

"How can I learn to trust You more?"
"REMEMBER WHAT I HAVE ALREADY DONE."
"Lord, why do I have so much trouble believing You will heal me?"
"BECAUSE YOU DOUBT MY PROMISES TO YOU."
"Why do I doubt Your promises to me, Lord?"
"IT GOES BACK TO VALUES."
"Would You explain what you mean by "values?"
"YOU FEEL VALUELESS IN YOUR FAMILY. YOU FEEL VALUELESS EVERYWHERE. YOU FEEL YOU ARE NOT *WORTH* HEALING."

May 5

"YOUR HEALING SHOULDN'T BE THE MOST IMPORTANT THING IN YOUR LIFE.
"Lord, would I find healing if I focus on my relationship with You?"
"YOU WILL FIND REST, AND IN REST YOU WILL FIND HEALING."
"Would You please sum up what you are trying to show me?"
"I WANT YOU TO UNDERSTAND HOW YOU CAN BE HEALED IN THE MIDST OF THE REST. I SHOW YOU THINGS THAT NEED TO BE FIXED, BUT WHEN I SHOW YOU THOSE THINGS, THIS THROWS YOU OFF IN STAYING IN MY REST."
"Lord, are You saying that I need to stay there in the middle of Your rest and depend on You to fix it?"
"THAT IS THE ONLY WAY IT CAN BE FIXED."

"Are you saying I am not asking You for enough things?"

"YOU ARE ASKING, BUT NOT BELIEVING I WILL REALLY DO IT. I WANT YOU TO LEARN TO LET GO OF EVERYTHING."

May 12

"Jesus, if I'm in Your will, why do I feel depressed?"

"IT'S BECAUSE YOU FEEL DEFEATED. THIS FEELING COMES FROM YOUR OLD PROGRAMMING. TO YOU, LETTING GO MEANS GIVING UP.

"Lord, am I defeated?"

"YOU HAVE EXHAUSTED YOUR STRENGTH. THE MAIN THING I WANT YOU TO DO IS LEARN TO REST IN ME."

"Am I learning?"

"Why didn't You answer me?"

"YOU ARE AFRAID TO HEAR ME BECAUSE YOU ARE AFRAID YOU WILL BE DISAPPOINTED IF YOU DO."

"Why do You think I would be disappointed?"

"BECAUSE YOUR FEELINGS ARE LYING TO YOU. YOUR FEELINGS ARE MAKING YOU AFRAID TO HOPE FOR SOMETHING THAT IS NEVER GOING TO HAPPEN."

"What am I afraid will never happen?"

"ALL OF YOUR DREAMS. ALL OF YOUR DREAMS CAN COME TRUE, BUT YOU DON'T *BELIEVE* THEY WILL COME TRUE. YOUR FEELINGS WERE LYING TO YOU WHEN THEY TOLD YOU YOUR DREAMS *WON'T* COME TRUE.

"Lord, I feel out of control."
"WHEN YOU ARE OUT OF CONTROL, THAT MEANS I AM IN CONTROL."

She said, "Lord, You know the problem I'm having with all this. Can You make it clearer?" She said that somehow her old programming wanted her to feel numb, but Jesus wanted her to trust the light, which was a new feeling. The devil wanted her to feel her numbness as death. She even saw herself laying on an altar- a long stone- and she was on top of it. The light was shining all around her. She said the numbness made her feel like she was dead. When she asked Jesus if He had a word that described what was happening to her on the altar, He said, **"RELEASE."** She asked if her old programming was being released. He said, **"YOU ARE NOT GIVING UP. YOU ARE LETTING GO. YOU HAVE RELEASED IT."** He said the old feeling would try to get her to get up off the altar, and the name of that feeling was control. He said He just wanted her to chill out because He had everything under control.

On June 26, Jesus told Martha to put all her expectations on the altar. When she asked Him to help her visualize that, she saw herself bringing something to Him. It was like her arms were full of stuff. She was holding a basket that was overflowing and stuff was falling out. As she got closer to him, she began stepping on the stuff. It was strange- she didn't *want* the stuff, and yet she wanted to bring the stuff to Him. A lot of little stuff was falling out, but there was something there that was big. She asked Jesus what the big thing was that she was holding onto, but bringing to Him. He said,**"EXPECTATIONS."** The closer she got to Him, the harder it was to carry the basket and walk at the same time. She asked Jesus why she couldn't just put those things down. Why did she have to bring them to Him? He said,

"BECAUSE YOU WANT TO BRING IT TO ME." He told her He wanted her to bring *all* her worries and concerns to Him.

She asked, "Is there anything else that You want to tell me tonight?" He said, "IT IS NOT ABOUT WHAT YOU WANT. IT IS NOT ABOUT YOUR EFFORT, IT IS ABOUT WHAT YOU LET ME DO FOR YOU." She said, "What is the best way for me to let You handle this?" She saw herself carrying that big old thing, and she was afraid to let it go because she was afraid it would fall on her toes. Jesus said, "WILL YOU TRUST ME TO CATCH IT?" She dropped it. It was falling. It didn't fall on her toes, it fell on Jesus. When she asked if there was anything else He wanted to tell her, He said, "TRUST ME TO CATCH IT."

On July 19, Martha asked Jesus to define the word, "forgiveness." He said, "AS IF IT NEVER HAPPENED." She said, "Lord, how do I apply this to my relationship with my brother? Are You saying I need to just forget everything he has ever done?" Jesus said, "THAT IS WHAT I DID FOR YOU." "Lord, how do I do that? I'm human and You are God, and I can't just forget what he has done. Are You telling me to do something I can't do?" "YES." "Are You trying to tell me this is something I can only do with Your help?" He said that was correct and He wanted to help her forgive her brother.

He said that her unforgiveness was the thing that was keeping her from letting go of the past. He told her if she forgave her brother and her brother hurt her again, He would help her get through the hurt. She asked if it was possible to forgive somebody and still not like them. Jesus said it was.

He went on to tell her that He wanted His children to need Him. She asked if He was saying she didn't need Him enough. He said, "YOU NEED ME MORE THAN YOU ARE WILLING TO ADMIT." He also told her that she couldn't be healed of her past until she was willing to forgive her family.

On August 4, Jesus talked with Martha some more about forgiveness.

"DON'T FIGHT THE *FEELING* OF UNFORGIVENESS, FIGHT THE DEMON."
"Lord, would You explain that?"
"WHEN YOU THINK OF SOMETHING YOUR BROTHER HAS BEEN DOING TO YOU, THEN MAKE YOURSELF CHANGE YOUR THOUGHTS BY REBUKING IT. YOUR THOUGHTS ARE THE FEELINGS OF UNFORGIVENESS, AND YOU HAVE BEEN WASTING YOUR TIME TRYING TO CHANGE THE FEELINGS."

On August 11, Jesus told Martha she needed to put her rights on the altar. He said if she could give up her rights, she would be able to forgive.

In our session on September 1, Martha asked Jesus if she still had issues with unforgiveness. When He answered, **"YES,"** she asked if it was regarding her brother. Getting no answer, she asked, "Lord, why aren't You answering me?" Jesus said, **"BECAUSE YOU ARE SO STRESSED OUT, YOU CAN'T HEAR ME."** She asked, "Lord, can You put me at peace so that I can hear You?" Jesus said, **"GO AWAY."** She asked what that meant, and Jesus said He wanted her to go away in her mind. He said He wanted her mind to take a vacation, and she could do that by not focusing on anything. She asked, "Lord, are You saying You want me to let You be responsible for everything going on in my life right now?" He said that He did, that she was trying to deal with too much.

October 26. Martha was angry when she came. She asked, "How can I concentrate on the Spirit when the world has tangled me up the way it has? How can I concentrate on the Spirit when my children are going hungry and they are cold? How can I concentrate on the Spirit when our family finances don't get straightened out?"

"SEEK YE FIRST THE KINGDOM OF GOD AND THESE OTHER THINGS WILL BE ADDED UNTO YOU."
"Lord, are You willing to bless my family?"

She said what she was getting was that, in the natural, she saw the *facts*. If she could go up in the spiritual, she would see the *truth*. She asked, "Lord, have You begun a good work?" He said He had, in her and in her family.

"THE FACTS OUTWEIGH THE TRUTH. YOU CAN'T SEE PAST THE FACTS TO SEE THE TRUTH. THE TRUTH IS, I HAVE BEGUN A GOOD WORK."
"Lord, how do I get past the facts so that I can see the truth?"
"YOU HAVE TO MAKE THE TRUTH BIGGER THAN THE FACTS AND I AM THE TRUTH."

November 3. In this session, Martha asked Jesus to tell her why she was afraid to accept His love. He said that she wanted it, but was afraid of it because, she thought if she accepted His love, that would mean she trusted Him, and she was afraid to trust Him because if she did, she would be disappointed. Therefore, it was easier to not trust anybody.

She asked, "Lord is it true that if I truly, completely trust You, I will be disappointed?" Jesus told her that her natural mind would be disappointed. She said, "Are You saying I may be disappointed, but You will still provide?"

"MY THOUGHTS FOR YOU ARE FOR GOOD AND NOT FOR EVIL."
"Lord, if I trust You, will You take care of me and my family?"
"YES."

November 9

"Lord, have I been depending too much on myself?"
"YOU FEEL YOU *HAVE* TO DEPEND ON YOURSELF."
"Is it because I feel I can't depend on You to provide for us?"
"IN SOME AREAS."
"Could You tell me what areas You are talking about?"
"IN TAKING CARE OF YOUR FAMILY. LONELINESS AND ISOLATION. YOU SHOULD DEPEND ON ME TO TAKE CARE OF YOUR FAMILY"
"Lord, could You explain what You mean by those areas of lonliness and isolation?"
"YOU DON'T FEEL YOU HAVE ANYONE WITH WHOM YOU CAN SHARE YOUR STRUGGLES. YOU SHOULD BRING ALL YOUR CARES DIRECTLY TO ME. I WILL HELP YOU LEARN TO DO THAT. YOU CAN DEPEND ON ME."
"How can I develop the faith that I can depend on You?"

"FAITH COMETH BY HEARING AND HEARING COMETH BY THE WORD OF GOD."
"Lord, if I confess all my struggles to You and look to You to supply, will You do that?"
"IF YOU BELIEVE."
"Lord, I believe for others. Would You help me to believe for myself?
"YES."

On November 17, Jesus indicated that, because her faith was increasing, He was putting light into her inner being.

"Jesus, are You putting light into me so the darkness will leave?"
"DARKNESS CAN'T EXIST WHERE LIGHT REIGNS. DEATH CAN'T EXIST WHERE LIFE REIGNS, AND DECEIT CAN'T EXIST WHERE VICTORY REIGNS. I HAVE BEGUN A GOOD WORK IN YOU AND I AM WELL ABLE TO CONTINUE IT AS LONG AS YOU KEEP THE FAITH TURNED ON. YOU CAN KEEP IT TURNED ON THROUGH DISCIPLINE. YOU HAVE TO DISCIPLINE YOURSELF."

When Martha came on December 1, she said she felt something great was going to happen soon, that something was going to open up, but she had no clue as what that might be. When she asked Jesus if she was about to go to another level, she had a vision. She and Jesus were on a mountain.

Jesus was on one level and she was on another. She was trying to get to the level He was on, and, at first, she thought Jesus was looking away from her. Then, He turned and looked at her. He indicated He wanted her to come higher, but didn't tell her how. There was a flimsy rope bridge there, connecting the level she was on with the one Jesus was on. She said it looked like this was where doubt and faith came in. If she stepped out on the bridge, that would be exercising faith. It appeared some boards were missing on the bridge. She told Jesus she didn't think she could make it; He kept saying, **"TRUST."** When she asked if she should keep her eyes on Him instead of on the bridge, He said that would be how her faith would be increased.

"THIS IS WHERE THE FACTS AND THE TRUTH ARE. THE BRIDGE CAN'T HOLD YOU UP, BUT I CAN."

Martha stepped out on the bridge. Although the bridge was shaky, she was walking, looking at Him, holding onto the rope of the bridge. She said it was like she was concentrating on the bridge by holding onto the rope, but she forced herself to keep her eyes on Him. When she got about halfway across she looked back at the bridge. It seemed to be strong and smooth- not like it was to start with. She said that part was like a brand new bridge. When she asked Jesus if the bridge was becoming complete as she made each step watching Him, she tripped. She asked Jesus why she had tripped. He said, **"SO YOU WOULD LET GO OF THE BRIDGE."** She said as she had fallen, she had let go of the bridge, and that was what He wanted her to do. At that point, Martha was aware of a spirit on the bridge with her. When she asked Jesus what this spirit was, He said, **"I AM CONNECTING YOU WITH THE SPIRIT OF FAITH. WHEN YOU LET GO, THE SPIRIT OF FAITH GRABBED YOU."** Martha said now it was just a matter of walking the bridge and that was awesome. She could see the facts, and the facts were that the bridge was still not complete, but the truth was that Jesus was not going to let her fall. At the end of the bridge, it went up so steeply that Martha couldn't walk any further.

She asked, "Lord, how do I get up to You?" He told her she had to crawl, she had to stay on her knees. At that point, she was under the ledge where Jesus had been standing. Jesus was lying down, talking to her. He held out His hand to her, wanting her to come up where He was. The only way to do that was to hold His hand.

As Jesus pulled her up, she was cut by the sharp rock. She asked, "Lord why is this cutting me as You are pulling me up?"

"MARTHA, WHAT IS IT CUTTING?"
"Lord, it is cutting my flesh. Why is it cutting my flesh?"
"FLESH CAN'T BE WHERE I AM. THE FLESH THAT IS BEING CUT OFF IS PRIDE."
"Lord, are You saying I have pride?"
"ALL OF MY PEOPLE DO. ALL OF YOU FEEL YOU HAVE ACCOMPLISHED SOMETHING WHEN YOU GET WHERE I AM. I DON'T WANT PRIDE TO GET IN THE WAY."

Martha said she was understanding that when she remembered being cut, she would remember that it was grace that got her there.

She was on the ledge now, standing there, and He was talking to her. He said He would not heal the scratches. He wanted to leave them there so she could remember. He said, **"TRUST MY GRACE."** She asked what she had to do now that she was on this level. He pulled her to him. It was like He wanted to hug her, but that was a different kind of hug. He wanted the blood that was dripping from her scratches to touch Him. She said it seemed to be important that her blood be connected with Him. She asked if He could tell Her why this was important. He pulled her up to Him. His side, which was pierced, was like an open wound and her scratches were open. He was wanting to fuse them together and the only way that could happen was if they were close together. They couldn't stand apart at all. She said that as long as they stayed that way- almost like Siamese twins- the sores didn't hurt, but if she pulled away, they would be reopened.

Jesus said, **"YOU HAVE TO BE A PART OF ME AND I HAVE TO BE A PART OF YOU. YOU CAN'T JUST BE CLOSE TO ME."** Martha thought Jesus wanted her to hug Him, but He said that no, He wanted to hug her. He told her that it was *His* strength that would keep her close to Him.

On December 15, Jesus told her He had set her free but she was struggling to walk in that freedom. She said she was struggling to go forward, but everything around her seemed to be pulling her back. She asked Jesus why He was allowing those things to pull her back. He said, **"YOU HAVE COME TO DEPEND ON THOSE THINGS AROUND YOU. I WANT YOU TO KNOW THAT I AM THE ONE WHO WILL PULL YOU FORWARD."** Martha said it was like when she was at the top of the bridge and there was no physical way to get where He was unless He pulled her up. She said at this point in her life, there was no way she could do anything unless He did it for her. He had gotten her to the place where she knew there was no one around she could depend on. She was totally isolated in every area. She felt abandoned because there was no one she could talk with about it. Jesus was wanting to pull her into Him, but right now, she had so much hurt, there was a struggle going on. He kept saying, **"STAY CLOSER, STAY CLOSER"** and she was doing everything she could to stay closer, but negative things keep coming on her. She said, "Lord is there anything I need to do to get closer to You?" He said, **"I WANT YOU TO REST."** She asked how she was supposed to rest with all the turmoil that was going on. He said she needed to rest in the middle of turmoil. He had given her the rest, but she had to fight for it. When she asked how she was supposed to fight for her rest, He told her to just focus on who she was in Him. When she asked who she was in Him, He said, **"A NEW CREATION."** She then asked if she was a new creation, why didn't she *feel* like a new creation.

"THE ENVIRONMENT AROUND YOU IS MAKING YOU FEEL YOU ARE NOT A NEW CREATION."
"But, Lord, I can't change the environment around me, can I?"
"AS YOU CHANGE ON THE INSIDE AND ACCEPT WHO YOU ARE IN ME, THEN THE OUTSIDE WILL CHANGE."
"Lord, what is my next step in being more accepting in You?"
"THERE IS NO NEXT STEP. EVERYTHING I WANT YOU TO DO HAS BEEN DONE."

In the session on December 29, Jesus confirmed that she was beginning to trust Him, but there was still some fear about letting go. When she asked where the fear was coming from, Jesus told her that all fear comes from Satan.

He went on to say that if she abided in Him and He in her, she could walk like *He* walked here on earth. She asked if this was a gift He wanted to give her, and He said it was. When she asked what it would take in order for her to receive the gift, He said, **"YOU HAVE TO LEARN TO BE CONTENT IN WAITING FOR THE GIFT. YOU NEED TO WAIT, WATCH AND EXPECT."** He told her that she was moving in the direction of that gift.

2006 Sessions

In the session on January 6, Jesus told Martha that rejection was a burden she had carried all her life in some form. He said, **"IT HAS WALKED BEHIND YOU EVERYWHERE YOU HAVE BEEN."** When she asked if He wanted to release her from the spirit of rejection, she started having a vision. She saw herself walking down a long road and a black figure attached itself to her. She tried to shake it off. When she could get it to loosen its grip, it continued to walk behind her. When something else happened, it would grab her again. She shook it off and it continued to walk behind her. It kept waiting for her to get off guard and then it would jump on her again. She asked Jesus if He wanted to remove this rejection so that it couldn't keep grabbing her. Jesus said that He did want to remove it.

Martha was trying to turn around so she could face the rejection. In the past, she had tried to walk away from it. It had a grip on her and she couldn't turn around and face it so that she could see it for what it really was. She wanted to turn around and face it, but was afraid if she did, she would be hurt again. She asked Jesus if He would hold her hand and be with her while she turned around so she wouldn't be hurt. "Jesus, You do want me to see this, don't You?" He said He wanted her to see it, but *she* wasn't real sure she wanted to. She asked what would happen if she faced it. Jesus said it would have to loose its hold on her.

> "If I face it, will anybody be able to hurt me like I've been hurt in the past?"
> **"THERE WILL STILL BE HURT, BUT YOU WILL BE ABLE TO WALK AWAY FROM IT."**
> "Lord, are You saying I will still be hurt, but without lasting effects?"

"IT WON'T BE ABLE TO ATTACH ITSELF TO YOU."

She asked if there would be any kind of physical healing if she faced it. He told her that stress-related problems would go away. She asked about emotional healing, and He said there would be healing for her co-dependency problem. Then she asked about spiritual healing, and He told her she would be spiritually renewed.

"Lord, would You please give me the courage to turn and face this thing that has been bothering me for so long?"
"I HAVE NOT GIVEN YOU THE SPIRIT OF FEAR, BUT OF POWER."
"Lord, what should I do next?"
"MY GRACE IS SUFFICIENT. MY STRENTH IS MADE PERFECT IN YOUR WEAKNESS."
"What does that have to do with what we have been talking about?"
"MY GRACE WILL GET YOU TO THAT POINT."
"Lord, are You saying Your grace will remove the spirit of rejection?"
"NO. MY GRACE WILL REMOVE THE FEAR."
"Lord, have I lived with rejection on my back for so long that I won't know how to react when it leaves?"
"REJECTION HAS SCREWED UP YOUR PERCEPTION SO MUCH, YOU FEAR YOU WON'T KNOW HOW TO SEE THINGS. I AM REALLY TRYING TO FULFILL YOUR DREAMS. WITHOUT REJECTION, YOU

**WILL BE ABLE TO GO BACK TO THE WAY
THINGS WERE BEFORE."**

Martha said it *was* her will that that spirit of rejection leave her. She asked, "Now can I turn around?" She saw herself trying to turn around. She was so restrained physically she couldn't. Jesus told her it was the power of the darkness that was keeping her from turning. She said, "Power of darkness, I bind you and cast you out in the name of Jesus Christ." It let go and she went limp, like it was squeezing the breath out of her. She said, "Lord, will You help me to face this now so that I won't keep having to face it for the rest of my life?" Jesus said, **"GIVE ME YOUR HAND."** With Him holding her hand, she turned and looked and said, "Why, it's just a bag of hot air with a face mask! Lord, is this what has been putting the blackness on me all this time?" Jesus said, **"THIS *IS* THE BLACKNESS."**

She said, "Now that I have looked at it and seen what it really is, and what it has done, will You take it out of my life?" Jesus said He wanted to show her all the areas of her life this had affected. He also said, **"THE FEAR OF FAILURE HAS BEEN AFFECTED BY THE FEAR OF REJECTION."** Martha said she had been afraid to fail because she would be rejected again, which has kept her from pursuing things. She said if a person wouldn't let her do something, she interpreted that to mean they didn't like her. She felt she always had to be working on somebody else's problem so that she would be loved, but that wasn't love anyway.

When she asked Jesus why He had allowed all that to happen in her life, He indicated it went back to free will. When she asked why Jesus finally allowed her to be healed, He said, **"BECAUSE OF MY GLORY."** She asked Him if He was going to use this to His glory; He said, **"ISN'T THAT WHAT IT IS ALL ABOUT?"**

She asked Jesus if there was anything else He wanted to tell her, He said, **"POP THE BAG!"** And, she did.

When she came on January 11, Martha told me about someone she knew who had abused drugs, alcohol, and was guilty of sexual misconduct, and Jesus had zapped him and healed him almost instantly, similar to Paul's Damascus Road Experience.

"Lord, why did You heal him so quickly and it's taken so long for You to heal me?
"EVERY CROSS IS DIFFERENT, EVERY PERSON IS DIFFERENT, AND EVERY MINISTRY IS DIFFERENT."
"Lord, is it Your will that it has taken so long for me to break free? Is this a part of my personal cross?"
"IT IS NOT THE EMOTIONAL PART THAT IS A PROBLEM, IT IS THE ENDURANCE. I COULD HAVE DONE IT INSTANTLY, BUT BECAUSE OF THE TYPE OF MINISTRY I HAVE FOR YOU, YOU ARE GOING TO HAVE TO ENDURE. BECAUSE I HAVE BEEN PATIENT WITH YOU, YOUR ENDURANCE WILL HELP YOU TO BE PATIENT WITH OTHERS."

Jesus told her she had felt guilty she had not been instantly healed, and there were many others who felt the same way. Those are the ones she will be ministering to.

On January 19, Martha had a vision in which she saw herself spinning, going up. She asked what this signified to Him. He said, **"THERE IS GOING TO BE A FAST TURNAROUND. A LOT OF THINGS ARE GOING TO BE HAPPENING AND IT IS GOING TO BE FAST. YOU**

WILL FEEL YOU ARE IN A WHIRLWIND. DON'T BE SURPRISED WHAT HAPPENS NEXT." When she asked if she was going to start realizing some of the desires of her heart coming to pass, Jesus said, **"VERY QUICKLY!"**

On February 2, she asked Jesus what had caused her to lose sleep the night before. He told her it was anxiety. He said the anxiety was coming from Satan himself. Satan was trying to use anxiety to distract her from what she really needed to be focused on. Martha asked what she could do when Satan did those things. She had tried to bind Satan and cast him out in Jesus' name, but that didn't work, and reading the Bible and praying didn't work. Jesus said she should use the gift He had given her. He told her when those things came at her, He wanted her to visualize laying down in His arms.

"YOU HAVE TO PRACTICE RESTING IN ME. IF YOU DO THAT WHEN THINGS AREN'T GOING ON, IT WILL BE EASIER WHEN SATAN DOES COME AT YOU."

When Martha came on February 9, she told us about a vision she had had. In the vision, she saw a courtyard with trees. She was inside the courtyard and she started dancing in the air. She asked Jesus if He gave her the vision. When Jesus said He did, she asked what the courtyard symbolized. He told her it was a place of entrance. He said the trees symbolized privacy and beauty. Her being inside symbolized rest, and her dancing in the air symbolized freedom.

She asked if there was anything else in the vision that she had forgotten. She saw steps going into the courtyard, and at the back, doors. Jesus said the steps symbolized thankfulness. When she asked why there were two doors, Jesus said one was for going in and the other for coming out. He said it symbolized she could go in and come out anytime she pleased. He told her this was a place of intimacy. He said it was her private place, that no one else could enter. Martha said that it was like the Psalm— "enter into His gates with thanksgiving and into His courts with praise."

She could see herself going in the door. She was looking but did not know what she was looking for. Jesus said, **"YOU HAVE TO GO IN."** She walked past a beaded doorway and was standing in the middle of the room, but couldn't see what was in the room. It was a place she had never been before. She said it was like, when she was dancing, she stumbled into this room. Jesus said, **"YOU HAVE ENTERED INTO A NEW ZONE."** He said this was a different realm, a spiritual realm. Martha said she could see herself. She was bewildered. She asked Jesus if she was supposed to be there. He told her this place had been waiting for her. When she asked what she was supposed to do there, He asked, **"WHAT DO YOU WANT TO DO HERE?"** She asked if she was *supposed* to want to do something there and Jesus said, **"IT IS YOURS."** She asked why it was so foreign to her, and Jesus said, **"BECAUSE YOU HAVE NEVER EXPERIENCED ANYTHING LIKE IT."** He told her this was where He wanted her to be.

Martha asked if He would show her around. She said, "He's coming up to me, but it's like He came up to me *in the room*. He reached out and took my hand. It was like He had been waiting for me. He came out of the dark part of the room, where I couldn't see Him." She asked why He was standing in the dark part of the room. He said, **"I WANTED TO SEE IF YOU WERE GOING TO STAY."** She said, "Why did You think I might leave, Lord?" He said, **"FEAR OF THE UNKNOWN."** She asked if He had now healed her of her fear of the unknown, and He said He had. She had been dancing free in the courtyard, and when He took her hand, she started dancing again. Even though she didn't know what was there, she was still dancing like it didn't matter what was there.

The room was no longer dark, or foggy. When she started dancing, the fog left. There was a home there. It had a kitchen, a living room, bedrooms- like a little cottage. She was going around looking at everything and touching things. She said, "This is my new world!" She asked Jesus what all this meant. He said, **"IT IS YOUR NEW LIFE. IT HAS NOT BEEN TOUCHED BY ANYONE."** She asked if it was the new birth that the Bible talks about. Jesus said, **"YOUR NEW LIFE. IT IS EVERYTHING. IT DOESN'T BELONG TO ANYBODY ELSE."** She and Jesus continued to talk to each other. She was touching everything and He was propped up against the living room doorway. He was not saying anything; He was just watching her. She went up to Him and He held her. She became aware that the door was open. She wanted to close it. She went over and closed and *locked* it. She didn't want anything from the outside to come in. She also felt she didn't ever want to go out. She was afraid if she went out, she might not be able to find her way back in.

"Lord, if I go out, will I lose my way to come back in?"
"DO YOU *WANT* TO GO OUT?"
"Lord, are You saying I could stay here all the time?"
"YOU COULD."
"If I did that, how could I get things done in my earthly body?"
"I DID WHEN I WALKED ON THE EARTH; THIS IS A MINDSET THAT I'M TALKING ABOUT
"Lord, are You saying that I can set my mind to stay in this place and still do what I need to do on earth,

and, if I can, can You help me to learn how to do that?"

"AS YOU BECOME ESTABLISHED, IT WILL BE LIKE A NATURAL THING FOR YOU."

"Lord, am I becoming established?"

"YES."

"What does it mean to become established?"

"YOU HAVE TO CHANGE EVERYTHING."

"Lord, does that mean becoming like You?"

"A MOVING INTO WHERE I AM."

She said this was like His base of operation. This was His place of residency. He can go out, and He can come back in. He can come back the same way He went out. He comes back in through thankfulness and the courts of praise.

Martha said, "Lord, are You saying You want me to move into Your home with You?" He said, **"NOT IN THE SENSE THAT I WANT YOU TO MOVE YOUR STUFF INTO HERE."** She said, "I have no stuff. What are You talking about?" Jesus answered, **"THIS IS WHAT I'M TALKING ABOUT: OLD THINGS HAVE PASSED AWAY AND ALL THINGS HAVE BECOME NEW. YOU *CAN'T* MOVE YOUR OLD STUFF INTO HERE."** When she asked, "Lord, are You saying that everything here is new for me?" He said, **"WHEN YOU STEPPED INTO THIS NEW PLACE, THEN EVERYTHING ELSE VANISHED. IT CAN'T CONTROL YOU ANYMORE."**

Martha said the way she understood all this was like when a protective witness is given a new identity. He is safe from anybody knowing who he is, but he could still contact someone from his old life. She said that Jesus had given her a choice: She could have a completely new life, with everything completely uncontaminated and as long as she stayed there, she could come and go; or she could go back and pick up something from the past, and have a hard time getting back in, so her past still existed. Jesus confirmed to her that if she let it, her past could still control her. She said, "Lord, is my fear that I might let that happen coming from Satan?" Jesus said it was.

She said, "What if somebody rejects me, Lord? Will I allow myself to react the way I always have? I'm so afraid I will. Lord, will You give me the strength to keep those old things from affecting me? Jesus answered, **"IT WASN'T YOU THAT GOT YOU THERE. HOW DO YOU EXPECT YOU TO KEEP YOU THERE? IT GOES BACK TO YOUR RELYING ON ME. IT WASN'T YOUR ABILITY THAT GOT YOU THERE TO START WITH."**

Martha said she really didn't have to be afraid of rejection any more. If it was left up to her, she had *better* be afraid of it, but it was not left up to her. She asked if her healing was now complete. Jesus told her that she was free and nothing could touch that freedom. She said, "I am completely free! I can actually go around my family and church people and not be concerned about how they react to me! It's almost unbelievable! I don't have to fear rejection! Wow! I've got my new life! I really have a new life! He gave me an uncontaminated mind!" She said, "Lord, what do I do now?" She said it was like everything in the old life was dead and the control, the fear, the perceptions, the always seeing things through the old mindset were gone. She said she kept thinking of the verse that says because I have the spirit of Christ, I have the mind of Christ, so I have the feelings and thoughts of Christ. I don't have any thoughts of my own. She said, "Lord, do I share this with anybody, or do I keep it to myself?" He said, **"YOU DON'T HAVE TO GUARD IT ANYMORE. YOU ARE FREE TO SHARE THIS WITH ANYONE."**

As a counselor, I had seen a soul set free! After all this time, Jesus had completely freed Martha from her past. It was one of the most awesome moments of my life, to be a witness to her healing.

Although I felt she would need no more healing sessions, I asked her to come back in two weeks to let me know how things were going for her.

When Martha came back on February 22, she said she felt so light, she could almost fly. In our time together, she asked Jesus a few more questions. She asked if He was going to lead people to Himself though the freedom they saw in her.

"I'M GOING TO TOUCH LIVES THROUGH YOU, AND YET, YOU ARE GOING TO ENJOY THE FREEDOM."
"Lord, is this something You will do, and I don't have to do anything?"
"ALL YOU WILL HAVE TO DO IS PLAY."

He told her He just wanted her to live in the freedom He had given her. When she asked if there was anything else He wanted to tell her, He said, **"COME PLAY WITH ME."**

She said, "Lord, is the pressure I'm feeling coming from religion?" He said, **"RELIGION TELLS YOU TO BE INVOLVED IN THE WORKS."** She said, "So, that's where my pressure is coming from, and You want me to stay free from religion?" His final answer was, **"YES!"**

It appeared we had a little more work to do. She came back on April 6. She had a feeling of not belonging that was bothering her, and she had a vision of a dark image in the special place Jesus had given her. She had fasted seeking an answer, but none had come. This is from our transcript of that day. She and Jesus were in her special place.

"Lord, did we deal with the feeling of not belonging?"

"NO."
"Can we deal with it now?"
"WHY NOT?"
"Can You show me where this started?"
"IN YOUR PAST."

"I see myself walking up to my brothers in the garden and they start complaining because I am there. I shouldn't be there, so I walk away. Lord, is this where this feeling started?" **"YES."**

"It's like the feeling of rejection and the feeling of not belonging got tangled up. If I'm working, I'm supposed to be there, but if I'm not working, I have no right to be there.'

"YOU FEEL LIKE AN OUTSIDER WHEN YOU ARE NOT WORKING."
"Lord, do You want to heal me of this?"
"DUH!"
"*Will* You heal me of this?"
"YES."
"Can You do it right now? Lord, what is this black image I keep seeing?"
"IT'S A SPIRIT."

"It's in the form of a person. It's almost like it has been camouflaged. It didn't want to be found, but, when I went on a fast, I could see it. Lord, does this spirit have a name?

"PUPPY DOG."
"What is the significance of that name- puppy dog?"
"IT WAS A TAG-ALONG. IT TAGGED ALONG WITH REJECTION."

"Before I dealt with the spirit of rejection, the spirit of rejection told the tag along to stay put. Rejection wanted to use that as a way to come back into my life. Lord, could You take this puppy dog completely out of my life?"

"YES."
"Could You remove it right now, Lord?"

Jesus opened the door. "When I saw that thing was there, Jesus said for me to stay put on the couch. Now that I've spotted it, He gets up and tells me to stay still. He goes to the door and deals with it. All He wanted me to do was acknowledge it was there, and He was going to deal with it."

"Lord, why has it been so hard for me to let You deal with it?"
"THIS IS YOUR NEW AREA OF REST, AND IN RESTING, YOU HAVE TO STAY AT REST."
"Lord, is there anything else You want to tell me about this?"
"I'M PROUD OF YOU!"
"The image is leaving and I'm still sitting on the couch." "Jesus, is there anything else?"
"YOU ARE THE APPLE OF YOUR DADDY'S EYE!"

"Jesus is standing there, holding me."

18.

From Alpha to Omega

The Holy Spirit has taught me many things in working with people from John through Martha.

With God's help, each of us has to discover truth for ourselves. Over time, God has taught me the best way to discover truth is by asking probing questions. Some good questions to ask *ourselves* in our search for truth are, "Am I enjoying the *triumphant, joyous, fulfilling* life the Bible talks about? Has my journey become humdrum? Is it possible my church is not providing the true soul food I need to sustain me in my Christian walk? Is it also possible I am looking too much to my Minister and my church and not enough to my Maker to provide me with that Spiritual food I so desperately need to make it through this world? In addition, is it possible there is much more to the spiritual realm than I've realized or been taught?"

In His sermon on the mount, Jesus said, "*Ask*, and it shall be given you; *seek* and ye shall find; *knock* and it shall be opened unto you." (John 7:7) If our walk has become dull and dreary, maybe we're not asking the right questions of the right person, not seeking in the right place, or maybe we're just not knocking often enough.

Most of the really important things I've come to *believe* in my own Christian walk have been learned, not so much in my local church as in my directly questioning God and in the counseling we provide; having people take their tough questions directly to God, listen for His answers and then share the conversation so it can be documented.

While I realize there are no "cookie-cutter" universal answers which apply to everyone, I believe some of these truths have pretty much universal application. Here are some of those truths as God has revealed them to me:

Truth 1 We can move truth from our heads to our hearts by meditating

Many of the people with whom we work are Christians. They have "head knowledge" about God. The problem is they don't have that same knowledge (or knowing) in their heart, or in their gut. Sometimes they may even be able to believe God's promises for someone else, but have a problem believing those same promises for themselves.

Belief only becomes meaningful when we have that belief anchored deeply within us. Having a knowledge in our head will not change our day to day actions. Having a belief deep within our gut does.

How does one move things from a "knowing" to a "believing?" God told Martha that the way she could do it was by *meditating*. He told her she needed to learn to relax in Him, to stop doing so much reading and start *thinking*. He said she should balance her time between reading and allowing Him to teach her.

Truth 2 God reveals the *unknown* to us so we can be healed

Probably 85-90% of what God reveals to our clients as He brings healing is not from our client's *conscious* memory. For example, there is no question that the revealing of *any* ancestral bond in their family is something which no client has had any awareness of prior to God's revealing it. Generally, all they are aware of is an obsession or an over-reaction in certain situations which they don't understand. Many times, God has made clients privy to information about an ancestor, or ancestors they were not even aware of, much less aware of what the ancestor *did* that caused their family to be bound.

In addition, God has allowed many of our clients to experience what they were feeling when they were *in the womb*, and what was going on outside the womb, if either of these was traumatic. Certainly the *memory* of what happened to us in our mother's womb is not available to our *conscious* memory, nor are the events going on outside the womb. There is also no conscious memory of our birth experience. In addition, things which occur between birth and around 6 years of age are also *generally* not available to our *conscious* memory, especially if what happened was traumatic. This isn't to imply that traumatic experiences don't occur *after* the age of 6, because they do, but usually these *are* available to conscious memory. It's the *hidden* bondage and traumas of the past and their consequences which cause the most problems in our client's lives, and these are the things the Holy Spirit reveals so that healing can occur.

Truth 3 We were all with God before we were conceived

Because of what the Holy Spirit has revealed to clients, I have come to the conclusion we were all with God *before we were conceived* for the simple reason that any time we have had a client question if that was so, the answer has always been **"YES."** Sometimes, God has even revealed to clients *before they left Him and were conceived*, that He was sending them into a particular family *for a reason.*

Truth 4 God sometimes reveals our purpose as He brings healing

A number of times, God has also revealed to clients the *purpose* for which they were created. The story of Karen in the chapter on "Purpose" is an excellent example of this. Before we were conceived; while we were still with God, I believe we knew what our purpose was but, in the process of being in the womb for nine months and then going through the trauma of birth, we forgot who we are as well as His purpose for us.

Truth 5 The game of life is seeking to become the person God originally created us to be.

The game of life, then, is to find our way back to God and to becoming the person God *originally created us to be.* Every fiber of my being tells me we will never be *happier* or more *fulfilled* than when we are doing exactly what God created us to be and to do (in that order). We can rest assured that God has already provided all the gifts and talents needed to accomplish our reason for being. This is what makes His burden so *easy* for us.

Truth 6 The Pure in Spirit see things as they really are

I believe if we don't return to our original creation while we are on earth, we *will* return to that state at death *if* we have asked Jesus to save us while we are in our earthly bodies. At the beginning of the Sermon on the Mount, Jesus said something interesting that applies here, "Blessed are the pure in heart, for they shall see God." "Pure" is a totally *objective* state, unaffected by prejudices, or pre-conceived notions. God is truth, and *truth* is what we will see when our spirits are pure. In other words, when we are pure in spirit, we will see things *as they really are*.

Truth 7 Death is simply a transition

I have also come to know that death is neither an ending or a beginning, but simply a *transition* from our physical existence to a spiritual one. I believe this because our essence is *spiritual* and that part neither ends or begins at death. And, regardless of what we may think, the spiritual existence of our loved ones who have died isn't far away from those of us still living in our earthly bodies, although there's a tendency to think there's a great chasm between us. Certainly, there is no *physical presence* and there is no way for us to *communicate* with them, but, from what God has revealed as we have worked with clients, those who have passed on are *aware* of at least *some* of the things going on with us. Many times, when God reveals that clients are bound by an ancestral bond and they ask that the bond be broken, God has indicated that some of their loved ones who became aware of the bond *when they reached the "other side,"* had prayed that someone in their family on earth would ask that the bond be broken. (Matthew 16:19b ...and whatsoever thou shalt bind on earth shall be bound in heaven; and whatsoever thou shalt loose *on earth* shall be loosed in heaven.) After the bond was broken, the Holy Spirit then revealed that there was *rejoicing in heaven* over the fact that it had finally been broken.

In Hebrews 12:1, Paul speaks of a "great cloud of witnesses" which encompasses us. I'm not certain what or who composes this cloud of witnesses, but I believe at least *part* of the cloud are those we loved who have gone on to be with Him.

Truth 8 We are to pray for the dead if Jesus puts their names on our hearts

I don't know the *reason* for this, but it seems that, at times, God wants us to pray for someone who has died. In the chapter on Dreams, the story of Molly is an example of this. God told her to continue to pray for her dead divorced husband until he was released. In the chapter on Ancestral Bonds, Paul was told to repent for an ancestor seven generations back who had not known the Lord. When he questioned God about praying for the dead, God made it clear that if He causes the name of one dead to come into our mind, we are to pray for him. In the same chapter, there's the story of Jason who repented for an ancestor from back in the 1600's in Virginia who raped a black lady. Jesus told him it would be good for him to ask for forgiveness for his ancestor.

Truth 9 Christianity is letting Jesus love us.

Although Satan would have us think that Christianity is complicated, it's really simple. We have to learn to let Jesus love us. He loves us by our allowing Him to serve us- such as bringing salvation or healing, or taking our cares on Him, or guiding us through our day-to-day cares and worries. We make it complicated when we are unwilling to give Him *complete* control of our lives.

Truth 10 God wants us to enjoy the ride.

This is what He told Bill in the chapter on the Religious Spirit. Also, when He was working with Martha, he told her to come play with Him. I think that more than anything,

Jesus wants us to experience joy when we walk with Him simply because we enjoy His presence and His guidance for our lives.

If our Christianity is burdensome, it is not Christianity.

Truth 11 We need to embrace our limitations.

This is what God told Bill in the chapter on the Religious Spirit. As I've gotten older, I've come to realize more and more the truth of this. There are things I used to do that I can no longer accomplish. And yet, as I think on it, I realize there have *always* been limitations to what I could do. As an example, one of my desires as a basketball player was to dunk a basketball. Even in my best days, I had neither the height nor the jumping ability to do that. It was important back then that I realize I was never going to dunk a basketball and concentrate on doing the things I could do as well as I could.

Now, at the age of 75, I realize the foolishness of trying to hold on to my youth to the point I attempt doing many of the things I used to do. I need to embrace my inadequacies and do what I still can as well as I can.

Truth 12 We have to learn to give up control to God.

If there is a universal problem with becoming a true follower of Christ, this is it. We all seem to have a tendency to want to hold on to as much control of our lives as we can. I know that one of the reasons I held off becoming a Christian as long as I did was my belief that if I gave my life to God, He would send me to Africa to be a missionary to the pigmies, because that was the worst thing I could think of doing. I discovered later that thought came from Satan, because I've learned God doesn't make us do things for which He hasn't prepared us, or which we are unwilling to do.

Truth 13 Humility means total submission to God.

In Barbara's story in the chapter on Ancestral Bonds, she asked God to define the word "humility." He said, **"HUMILITY MEANS TOTAL SUBMISSION TO THE FATHER."** He went on to tell her that humility had nothing to do with her actions or with other people. He said, **"HUMILITY IS BETWEEN YOU AND ME. HUMILITY HAS TO DO WITH YOUR BEING UNDER MY AUTHORITY, NOT HOW YOU RESPOND TO SOMEBODY."**

Truth 14 God will provide for our needs and what we don't need won't make us happy.

This is also found in the chapter on Ancestral Bonds and is what God told the divorced lady who thought she was missing something by not being married and because she thought people looked down on her because of her unmarried state.

Truth 15 Jesus' strength is made perfect in our weakness, but we have to be willing to call on His strength.

Jesus is always willing to help us, *if we are willing to ask for that help.* As He told Martha, Satan cannot prevent Jesus' giving things to us, but he can prevent our accepting them. We don't accept His gifts when we don't ask.

Truth 16 If we want to learn to trust Him more, we have to remember what He has already done.

A good exercise when our faith wavers or when we are depressed is to get a piece of paper and ask Him to remind us of all the positive things He has already provided. Usually, before we have the page half-filled, our faith is strengthened.

Truth 17 What we do for Him is not as important as what we let Him do for us.

This is a truth that helps us to get things in perspective. If we get it deeply within us, it will change our life.

Truth 18 Don't fight the *feeling* of unforgiveness- fight the demon.

This is what He told Martha when she was having so much trouble forgiving her brother. He told her forgiveness is *not* a feeling, so it's a waste of time to work at changing the feeling. We need to work on the demon of unforgiveness. When the thought of what someone has done to us comes into our minds, we need to change our thought by rebuking that thought and casting it out in the name of Jesus Christ.

Truth 19 We have to be part of Jesus and He has to be a part of us. We can't just be close to Him.

This is another truth He explained to Martha. This ties in with the truth made clear in the book of John, where Jesus says, "I am the true vine, you are the branches. Without me, you can do nothing."

Truth 20 Every Cross is different, every person is different and every ministry is different.

This is the reason it is the height of folly for us to compare ourselves with anyone else. One problem with our comparing ourselves to others is that we tend to compare what we consider to be the *best* in others with what we consider to be the *worst* in us. When we compare ourselves with others, we always come out the loser.

Truth 21 All God's Children Have a Problem With Pride

This is what the Holy Spirit told Martha, and the statement has the ring of truth about it. We all tend to feel that we have brought ourselves to the place where we are in Him. When we do that, we forget that He created us, gave us the gifts and talents that we have, and placed a longing in us that is never satisfied until we find a relationship with Him.

One of the extreme examples of Christian pride is found in some people in the charismatic movement. In that movement, those who had been given the gift of speaking in tongues often made the statement that, unless one had the gift of tongues, they had not received the anointing of the Holy Spirit. They went about trying to teach people how to receive this gift. This is a gift that Paul said was the least of the gifts and that it was divisive.

Truth 22 Healing takes more than just removing bad programming

In thinking about any therapy that only removes bad programming and doesn't build back anything in the empty space that's left, I'm reminded of the words of Jesus found in Luke 11:24-26, "When the unclean spirit is gone out of a man, he walketh through dry places, seeking rest; and finding none, he saith I will return unto my house whence I came out. And, when he cometh, he findeth it swept and garnished. Then goeth he and taketh to him seven other spirits more wicked than himself; and they enter in, and dwell there: and the last state of that man is worse than the first."

If what Jesus said is true, and there is absolutely no doubt in my mind that it is, just removing bad programming from people's lives doesn't complete the job. When the bad programming is removed, the space it occupied *must* be filled with the Holy Spirit, or the problems that come will be worse than people had when they first came for healing.

19.

Does it Always Work?

D on't you just love being asked a good question? Seeking the answer to a good question can bring new truth. A friend recently asked me, "Does what you do *always* work?" Without giving it much thought, I said, "Of course not." But, his question got me thinking about what the answer to that *should* be. I recalled that when Jesus was in His earthly ministry, his healings were the most dramatic things He did. He provided healings for all kinds of problems. In some situations, we are told that many people came for healing and He healed *every one of them*. These miraculous healings got people's attention and drew multitudes to Him. But when you think about it, you realize that no matter how dramatic His healings were, which even included raising people from the dead, all the people He healed or raised from the dead eventually died. No matter how dramatic His healings were, they were only of a *temporary* nature. The really important work of His ministry was to point people to God. By looking at Jesus, people were better able to understand the true nature of God and receive *spiritual* healing, which is forever.

Because of my friend's question, and the revelation that came from considering it, I've come to a different understanding about the mission of our ministry. For almost 20 years now, I've thought the most important part of our work has had to do with bringing emotional healing to hurting people, and some of these healings have been dramatic, as I hope you've seen in some of the case histories we've shared. Until now, it's been disappointing that so many people have come to us for only a few sessions. Because of my friend's question and God's revelation about the true mission of our ministry, I've come to realize that the most important thing we do is to let people know that God wants to speak directly with them. Hopefully, our work is an important first step in helping people recognize God's voice and realize He wants to have a personal relationship with them.

Any emotional healings our ministry has assisted with have hopefully helped make life more bearable for those involved, but these healings won't count for much unless what we have done has helped our clients have a closer walk with God.

If I were asked the same question again, "Does what you do always work," I would honestly have to say, "I don't know." The reason I don't know is because I seldom know the end of the story. What we do is, of course, only a part of the healing God provides. Only God knows the final answer to the question of whether it works. One reason I have a different outlook is because of something that happened recently involving a lady I worked with over ten years ago.

The lady was very concerned about her young son. She only came for two or three sessions. I honestly thought we had been of no help to her. This experience with her has been a good lesson for me that, although we may see no evidence of it, God continues with any healing He starts. There are obviously times when all He wants us to do is get the ball rolling, and He handles the healing in His own time, in His own way, as He did in this instance.

This lady told me we could quote from her recent letter.

Dear Charles,

I wanted you to know how much your sessions with me several years ago meant to me and my family. You will remember I came to you with my son Joe's depression. It was through you that I first heard about spiritual bondage and came to understand its influence on my family and me. Joe's depression was severe. There were times when he was nearly catatonic and was not able to get off the couch. He stopped growing physically.

When our child hurts or is sick, we want them healed (restored) quickly. Like most mothers, I wanted instant answers and instant healing. Instant healing didn't happen and I struggled with that. After our session, God provided a wonderful Christian physician/children's psychiatrist- a rare bird, who agreed to counsel Joe.

The changes in my life and Joe's that happened over the last seven years could not have taken place if the spiritual groundwork had not been laid. The bondage has been broken for me and for my family and the healing has reached into areas of my life that I didn't know needed to be reworked.

During my session with you, we named two bondages in my family, one for the woman named *rebellion* and a bondage for the men we did not need to name for the bondage to be broken for all who accepted the gift. At the end of my session, you said you thought the men's bondage was sexual. Before my Dad died recently, he asked a friend to get rid of his stash of pornography. I watched his friend make two trips carrying several large black garbage bags out of Dad's bedroom. After Dad died, we carried another large bag out of the house.

Settling the estate has been an enormous task and it has been a hard couple of years with the family in turmoil, but the bondage is broken for me and the healing continues. I wanted to bring you up to date on where we are as a family and the final gift. Joe's psychiatrist dismissed him last Thanksgiving. He has not needed any medication for about a year. Joe plans to participate in a mission trip to Africa this summer. This is the child we thought would not be able to attend public school or hold a job.

Already the child who struggled with that hard question of "*Why did God make me go through this?*" has shared his story and God's gracious gift with another who needed to know they weren't alone.

When I wrote back, I told her that I had honestly felt our ministry had not been of any help at all to her or to Joe and, for that reason, her letter was especially appreciated. Although we have experienced many instances of ancestral bonds being broken, we seldom get feedback on the results. Her letter and the encouragement we got from it was very special and meaningful to us.

20.

The Most Important Thing

When we are working with clients, we give them the questions to ask God and then ask that they get quiet and listen for God's answers. Unless we are aware of a special need of a client, we usually start with an open-ended question such as, "Lord, where would You like for me to start today?" The next question depends on the answer to the first question, and generally seeks more information about the first answer. We keep asking questions in this way until we get down to what clients need in order to find direction and healing.

There's a saying that goes, "The most important thing is keeping the most important thing the most important thing." As in our counseling, this statement brings up the next question, "What is the most important thing?"

When clients are frustrated, confused, or hurt and ask what they should do next, the most important thing seems to be that they should, **"KEEP YOUR EYES ON JESUS,"** or **"KEEP YOUR EYES ON GOD,"** because this is the most frequent answer Jesus gives.

This answer implies that more is required than just *occasionally* looking to Jesus or to God to help us. It means more than seeking help from Jesus only when there are major problems in our lives. "Keep" means "constant, ongoing," so the inference is that keeping our eyes on Jesus should be, not an *occasional* happening, but an *ongoing* lifestyle.

The Bible provides an excellent example of a person's taking his eyes off Jesus. Most of us are familiar with the life of Peter, the disciple Jesus named "The Rock." Peter was a fisherman. He and his brother Andrew were the first two disciples called to "become fishers of men." Peter was there when Jesus preached the sermon on the mount. He was there when Jesus went about healing and raising people from the dead. Once, when Jesus went to Peter's house and found his wife's mother sick, He touched her and healed her fever. Peter was there when Jesus calmed the tempest. He was one of the 12 sent out to preach that the kingdom of heaven was at hand, and one of those to whom Jesus gave the power to heal the sick, cleanse the lepers, raise the dead, and cast out devils. When Jesus walked on the sea, Peter was the *only* disciple who had the faith to attempt to walk out to Him on the water. He was with Jesus at the last supper. The point is, Peter was one of Jesus' top disciples who Jesus was counting on to help carry on His ministry after His death.

The book of John tells of a time late in Jesus' earthly ministry when He told Peter that, unless he changed his *attitude*, he could no longer be a part of Jesus' ministry, and, at first glance, it appears to be over a rather insignificant event. Let's look at the story. It's found in John 13:4-9.

> He (Jesus) riseth from supper, and laid aside his garments; and took a towel and girded himself. After that he poured water into a bason (basin), and began to wash the disciple's feet, and to wipe them with the towel wherewith he was girded. Then cometh he to Simon Peter: and Peter saith unto him, Lord, dost thou wash my feet? Jesus answered and said unto him,

What I do thou knowest not now; but thou shalt know hereafter. Peter saith unto him, Thou shalt never wash my feet. Jesus answered him, If I wash thee not, thou hast *no part* (my emphasis) with me.

If you are familiar with the story, you know what comes after that. "Simon Peter saith unto him, Lord, not my feet only, but also my hands and my head."

What was so terrible about his reaction to Jesus' washing his feet that caused Jesus to say that unless Peter allowed Him to wash his feet, he could have *no part* with Him? Here was a man who had followed Jesus from the beginning, and as far as we know, did everything Jesus ever asked him to do to this point. Why was it so *important* to Jesus that Peter allow Him to wash his feet? The answer is, Peter has not learned to let Jesus *serve him. Peter had taken his eyes off Christ and was seeing the situation as the world sees it.*

The truth of this came through clearly to me recently as I was reading Dr. Dennis F. Kinlaw's outstanding book, *Every Christian Can Have The Mind of Christ*. After discussing the foot washing episode, Kinlaw made this radical statement: *If you are offended by the idea of Jesus being your servant, you have the same problem Peter had. You still think as the world thinks, not as God thinks."* (emphasis mine) (Kinlaw, p 42, used with permission, Evangel Publishing House)

Allowing Jesus to be our servant is "thinking as God thinks." If Jesus could say to Peter, that if he didn't let Jesus serve him, he could have no part of Him, how much more is He saying to us, *"If You are not willing to let me serve you, then you are separating yourself from me."*

Washing His disciples' feet had nothing to do *directly* with the any of the reasons Jesus came to earth, but it had everything to do with the *attitude* Jesus knew His disciples had to have in order to carry on His ministry. He knew what those of us know who have ever been a part of a foot washing ceremony. It's relatively *easy* to wash someone else's feet, but it is *extremely humbling* to allow someone to wash ours. *It takes a humble spirit to allow Jesus to serve us.* It takes the same humble spirit to follow and serve Him.

In the seventeenth century, there was a French monk named Brother Lawrence, who learned to practice the presence of God *at all times*. The following is from his writings, *The Practice of the Presence of God*. The book came from conversations he had with a superior, who wrote down the things they discussed:

> "That we ought to act with God in the greatest simplicity, speaking to Him frankly and plainly, and imploring His assistance in our affairs, just as they happen. That God never failed to grant it, as he (Lawrence) had often experienced.
>
> That he had lately been sent into Burgundy, to buy the provision of wine for the society which was a very unwelcome task for him, because he had no turn for business, and because he was lame and could not go about the boat but by rolling himself over the casks. That, however, he gave himself no uneasiness about it, nor about the purchase of the wine. That he said to God it was His business he was about, and that he afterward found it very well performed.
>
> So, likewise, in his business in the kitchen (to which he had naturally a great aversion), having accustomed himself to do everything there for the love of God, and with prayer, upon all occasions, for His grace to do his work well, he had found everything easy, during fifteen years that he had been employed there.

That he was very well pleased with the post he was now in; but that he was as ready to quit that as the former, since he was always pleasing to himself in every condition by doing little things for the love of God.

That with him the set times of prayer were not different from other times; that he retired to pray, according to the directions of the superior, but that he did not want such retirement, nor ask for it, because his greatest business did not divert him from God."
(Lawrence, p 19-20, Baker Publishing Group)

In several of the case histories, Jesus showed how it is possible to be active in the world and, at the same time, not be part of it. He showed these clients that there is a place within where they can go to grow and be with Him in good times so that, when things in their lives get rough, they can retreat into that special place and find peace. He told Martha it was a "mindset."

From what Jesus has revealed to some of our clients and confirmed by other Christian writers, it's obviously very important for every believer to ask Jesus to help them find this special place within.

Jesus also told Martha, **"IT IS NOT ABOUT YOUR EFFORT. *IT IS ABOUT WHAT YOU LET ME DO FOR YOU.*"** Allowing Jesus to serve us includes asking Jesus to help us with things we normally think of as insignificant. For example, years ago, the Holy Spirit led me to start praying for parking spaces. The first time I did this was at the Macon Mall the day before Christmas. When my wife Mary and I were entering the parking lot at the Mall, we could see that cars were chock-a-block all over the parking lot. I told Mary we needed to pray for a parking space. I didn't actually pray for it other than mentioning that we should. We drove down the lane leading to the entrance where we wanted to go in. As we turned just opposite that entrance to go back up the next lane, a man I'd never seen before came running out of the entrance, waving his arms at us. When I let the window down, he said, "Are you looking for a parking space?" When I told him we were, he told me he was parked right in front and would hold the space for us until we could go around. When we got back around, he pulled out, and we parked just opposite the entrance we wanted to go in. In telling some friends about it later, I told them I hoped the fellow had finished his shopping before God told him to come out and give us his space.

Since then, I almost always pray for parking spaces. Most of the time, I get the space I want, but, even when I don't, my faith is not shaken. I've finally come to the conclusion that the *important* thing is not getting the parking space, but letting one of my more insignificant needs cause me to think of Jesus and to ask for His help.

So, Jesus is anxious to do what we consider to be little things for us- like providing parking spaces, or helping us find lost objects. No request is too small, or too large for Jesus. He is just waiting to be asked. *He wants us to continually be aware of His presence with us.*

Because of what He has shown us through the incident of the foot washing with Peter, the witness of Brother Lawrence, and His witness to many of our clients, I've now come to the conclusion that it may possibly be that *the most important thing is to make Jesus so much a part of our lives that we ask His help in all things and include Him in everything we do.* He should be such a part of our days that we are constantly talking with Him and seeking His direction for even our most menial tasks. Out of our allowing Him to serve us will come: Faith, Hope, Love and many other good things. As we learn to allow Him to serve us in every part of our lives, it becomes easier and easier to allow Him to serve us in the really major issues of life.

The *only* reason Self/Rise exists today is because Jesus desires to serve hurting people. He has served them through His willingness to use this Ministry as, through the working of the Holy Spirit, He has provided counseling, healing direction and anything else our clients have needed in order to be made whole...

...and He *continues* to do that.

LaVergne, TN USA
22 January 2011
213563LV00002B/1/A